WHAT A WAY TO TRAVEL

Visiting over 60 countries

WHAT A WAY TO TRAVEL

Visiting over 60 countries

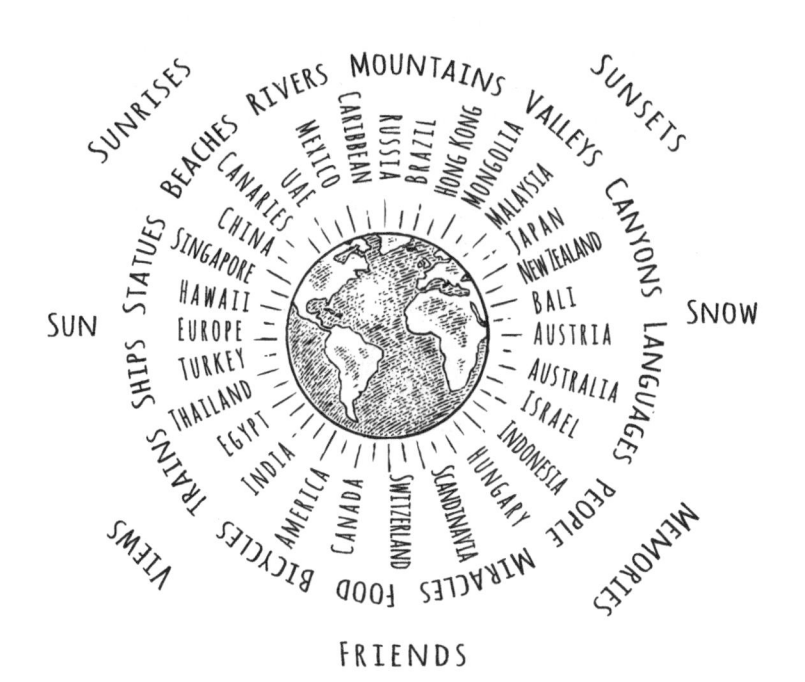

SUNRISES · BEACHES · RIVERS · MOUNTAINS · VALLEYS · SUNSETS
CARIBBEAN · RUSSIA · BRAZIL · HONG KONG · MONGOLIA · MALAYSIA
MEXICO · UAE · CANARIES · JAPAN · NEW ZEALAND · CANYONS
SUN · STATUES · SINGAPORE · CHINA · BALI · LANGUAGES · SNOW
SHIPS · HAWAII · EUROPE · AUSTRIA · AUSTRALIA · PEOPLE
TRAINS · TURKEY · THAILAND · ISRAEL · INDONESIA · MEMORIES
VIEWS · BICYCLES · FOOD · EGYPT · INDIA · AMERICA · CANADA · SWITZERLAND · SCANDINAVIA · HUNGARY · MIRACLES

FRIENDS

BRANDON SHACKELL

BROWN DOG BOOKS

First published 2023

Copyright © Brandon Shackell 2023

The right of Brandon Shackell to be identified as the author of this work has been asserted in accordance with the Copyright, Designs & Patents Act 1988.

All rights reserved. No part of this book may be reproduced, stored in a retrieval system, or transmitted in any form or by any means, electronic, electrostatic, magnetic tape, mechanical, photocopying, recording or otherwise, without the written permission of the copyright holder.

Published under licence by Brown Dog Books and
The Self-Publishing Partnership Ltd, 10b Greenway Farm, Bath Rd, Wick, nr. Bath BS30 5RL

www.selfpublishingpartnership.co.uk

ISBN printed book: 978-1-83952-612-1

Cover design by Kevin Rylands
Internal design by Andrew Easton

Printed and bound in the UK

This book is printed on FSC® certified paper

MIX
Paper | Supporting responsible forestry
FSC
www.fsc.org
FSC® C013604

COVERING

- Over 60 different countries
- Thirty years of on-off travelling adventures
- From a tandem bicycle to a cruise liner – the QE2
- True life stories from diaries written at the time of visit
- Capturing feelings, emotions, sights, sounds and smells
- Plus humour and strange incidents and happenings
- Featuring Europe, Asia, Australia, The Americas (North and South), Africa, Scandinavia, Caribbean and Indonesia
- New and old Wonders of the World
- The best beaches in the world
- The people you meet and befriend while travelling

JOIN BRANDON JACK SHACKELL (BRAD) ON THIS MYSTERY TOUR AND DISCOVER ANOTHER WORLD TO THAT OF YOUR OWN, INCLUDING DIFFERENT CULTURES AND WAY OF LIFE

FOREWORD

It has been said before ...

'Never judge a book by its cover'

The same must be said about people...

'Never judge people by their clothing or appearance'

This is my advice after travelling around the world for over 30 years: people will never stop surprising or amazing you.

I have slept under the stars, in airports, outside airports, in tents or first-class cruise liners and some of the best and worst hotels in the world.

Not only does travelling broaden your mind, it becomes an adventure and memories and experiences which last you a lifetime.

But more important than the sights and views are the lifetime friendships you make and the people you meet during your travels.

DEDICATED TO:

My mum and dad who gave me my start and inspiration to travel.

My family and friends who were a vital part in accompanying me on the travels.

With a special mention for Steve who gave me so many laughs and memories.

With a special acknowledgement and message to Lucy, Ellis & Becky, my nieces, Danny and James, my nephews, in the hope that one day they will read these pages, leading them to feel so inspired that hopefully they walk and stand in my footsteps around the world.

Also a profound thank you to everybody around the world who showed me warmth, happiness and friendship and when I most needed it, help, advice and information.

Last but not least you, being the person reading this book, I hope it gives you as much joy as it did me to write it, reliving my adventures, trips and travels.

CONTENTS

MY MEMORIES OF THE FIRST TRIP ABROAD	21
SWITZERLAND	22
CAN YOU RIDE A TANDEM? YEAH, OF COURSE.	26

BUT AS FAR AS FRANCE, BELGIUM AND EVEN LUXEMBOURG?

PARIS, FRANCE	29
SPAIN	33

MAJORCA/ COSTA DEL SOL/ MALAGA/TORREMOLINOS/ MARBELLA/ COSTA BRAVA/BARCELONA/ COSTA BLANCA/ ALICANTE/ BENIDORM/ IBIZA/ SANTA EULALIA/ CALA LLONGA/ IBIZA TOWN/FORMENTERA/ GRAN CANARIA/ TENERIFE

THE HONEYMOON AND STILL WANTED TO TRAVEL	40

BELGIUM/ GERMANY/ AUSTRIA/ ITALY/ VENICE/MARINO/ SWITZERLAND

CRUISING THE MEDITERRANEAN	49

ITALY - VENICE/YUGOSLAVIA - DUBROVNIK/GREECE - ATHENS - MYKONOS - RHODES - SANTORINI - DELPH/TURKEY - KUSADASI - EPHESUS/CYPRUS/ISRAEL - JERUSALEM - BETHLEHEM/EGYPT - CAIRO – GIZA

HOLLAND – AMSTERDAM	67
GRAND TOUR OF FRANCE	71
AMERICA – USA	79
THE AMERICAN WEST	92
CRUISING THE CARIBBEAN	106
BRAZIL - SOUTH AMERICA	121

FROM HARLOW TO HONG KONG	128
THE NETHERLANDS, WEST AND EAST GERMANY, POLAND, RUSSIA INNER AND OUTER MONGOLIA, CHINA, HONG KONG	
AROUND THE WORLD IN 28 DAYS	165
STOPPING AT USA - LOS ANGELES, MEXICO, HAWAII - HONOLULU, NEW ZEALAND - AUCKLAND, AUSTRALIA - SYDNEY, THAILAND BANGKOK, PATTAYA (VIA INDIA), LONDON	
INDIA - JAPAN – INDIA	196
DELHI - AGRA - DELHI - TOKYO - HIROSHIMA - KYOTO - TOKYO - DELHI – LONDON	
WALES, IRELAND, EIRE, WALES, THE ISLE OF ANGLESEY	220
SCOTLAND	228
GUERNSEY – CHANNEL ISLANDS, HERM, JERSEY	233
FRANCE - PARIS/ANDORRA/SPAIN/PORTUGAL - LISBON - THE ALGARVE/SPAIN - SEVILLE - GIBRALTAR/MOROCCO - TANGIERS, RABAT, CASABLANCA	236
ACROSS EUROPE FRANCE/GERMANY/CZECHOSLOVAKIA - PRAGUE/AUSTRIA - VIENNA	257
BRATISLAVA/HUNGARY - BUDAPEST/YUGOSLAVIA/DENMARK - COPENHAGEN/SWEDEN – MALMO	
LIVING ABROAD	283
ITALY - PERUGIA/AMERICA – ORLANDO	
THE OLD ANCIENT WONDERS OF THE WORLD	286
MY PERSONAL CHOICE OF THE NEW WONDERS OF THE WORLD	
FUTURE TRIPS TO PLAN	292

We all live in this universe, which we cannot really see or feel or smell, but we can do all of these things within the world we live in, so for those people who have never been inspired to travel, or who have been to Spain once or Majorca, I am going to attempt to give you a flavour of what is actually out there, in the hope that one day you will hopefully want to broaden your horizons.

Have I always wanted to travel, was I meant to be a traveller or was I of a nomadic existence in a previous life? Who knows?

My start in travelling was probably a stroke of luck as I was ten years old and still at junior school when the pupils were offered a ten-day cruise to Scandinavia, visiting Norway, Denmark and Sweden. At the time mum was a cleaner, and dad being a semi skilled worker and with eight children times were tough. My mum read the form and asked me if I wished to go. I answered 'Yes' with so much excitement and wonderment that my mum scrimped and saved to obtain the money required for the trip.

The year was 1963 and the cost in total was about £40:00 and, of course, I needed a few new clothes and a little case which I could manage to carry. Once sorted, that was it. I was going and just had to wait for the off!

What goes through a ten-year-old boy's mind? Anticipation mixed with excitement and fear, having never before been away from home and all that is familiar. The day eventually arrived and, what with very little sleep the night before, I was up and raring to go. The family walked me down to the local school and then it was all about kisses and farewells. Have a good trip. Do as you are told by the teachers. Take care. Be careful, don't do anything silly or play up. Those goodbye tears still bring a lump to my throat.

And I am off. This is it, I have got my new black case with my name written on it, a little old plastic camera and about 30 school chums and we are going to have a blast.

The first 30 minutes we were all a little quiet, I reckon the farewells and waving goodbye had taken their toll.

Also the teachers were now bombarding us with the 'Do's and Don'ts' and when the coach stops you must all line up outside the vehicle, now put all your name tags on then, kids being kids, the excitement really started. Giggling, having fun and generally doing all the things children are experts at.

Once we had all got off of the coach, there she stood, the 'MS DEVONIA'. We walked along the gangplank and we were on board.

We ran everywhere, upstairs, downstairs, opened cupboards, closed them, got inside of them, touched everything, picked it up, moved it, nothing was safe from our grubby little fingers, even the windows had sticky marks on, or where a tongue, nose or hot breath had been pushed and breathed against it.

A klunk and a whirling noise, the anchor was being lifted and we were about to set sail for distant waters and exciting lands.

Now remember, I was just ten years old when I was on this trip so the travel details are not comprehensive, but fear not, I do return to Scandinavia later on and am able to go more in-depth later in this book. My child memories are:

WHAT A WAY TO TRAVEL

PORT	HOURS IN PORT	COMPETITION (AWARDED FOR)
Liverpool		
Bergen (Norway)	18	
Gothenburg (Sweden)	13	
Copenhagen (Denmark)	15	

Essays – best kept logbook – sketches Games – best kept dormitory
Best kept scrap book

QUESTIONS TO ANSWER
BERGEN
MY ANSWERS

Q: What were the streets like, cobbled or paved? Were the buildings different in any way from those at home? Did the traffic drive on the right or the left?
How many British cars did you see?
Name some of the foreign makes of car that you saw. How much did it cost to send a postcard to Britain? How were the children dressed?
How were their parents dressed? How were the old people dressed?
Was there anything unusual about the houses? What articles did you buy and what did you pay?

WHAT A WAY TO TRAVEL

A: They were cobbled and paved. Yes they were in every way.
On the left.
I saw two cars of Britain's. Ford, Jaker [Jaguar]
It cost 6d to send.
They were dressed in macks. The same as the children.
With very old macks on. Yes there was.
I buyed two seals and they were five krona each.

NEEDLESS TO SAY, I DID NOT WIN THIS COMPETITION OR ANY OTHER.

DO NOT
- a) Sit on the ship's rails
- b) Climb on the superstructure
- c) Tamper with the ship's gear
- d) Slide down the centre rail of the staircase
- e) Run in the corridors
- f) Put heavy paper/cartons, apple cores or any other bulky objects into the lavatories
- g) The girls' dormitories are out of bounds at all times to the boys and vice versa.

INFORMATION SUPPLIED TO US FROM SCHOOL

NORWAY

Norway is situated in the Western and Northern part of the Scandinavian Peninsula. The sea surrounds it on three sides. The capital is Oslo.

WHAT A WAY TO TRAVEL

The Lapps, who live in the North, are quite distinct from the Norwegians, their country is Lapland, extends across Norway, Sweden, Finland and part of Russia.

BERGEN

On the West Coast of Norway, in a sheltered bay protected from the open sea by several islands. The name 'Bergen' means, 'pasture among the mountains'.

100 ORE = 1 KRONE

Places to note
Old Bergen (Museum) Churches
The Old City Hall The Old City Gate Fish Quay Rosenkrantz Tower The aerial Cableway Grieg's home

Do you speak English?
Yes No
Thank you How much?
Where is the toilet? Please

Swaller de Engelisk?
Ya
Nei Mangetakk Mvormye?
Mvor er toalettet?
Damer-Ladies/Herrer-Gentlemen Vennligst

WHAT A WAY TO TRAVEL

SWEDEN
Capital is Stockholm, largest of the Scandinavian countries.

GOTHENBURG one of Sweden's important ports which is ice free in winter.

100 ORE = 1 KRONA

Places to note:
Guston Adolf Square Harbour of Lilla Bommen Trolleybuses and buses Stadium

Do you speak English?
Please Thank you How much?
Where is the toilet? Have you any?
Stamps Postcards Ice cream

Talar ni Engelska?
Var god
Tack sa mycket Hurmycket?
Var ar toiletten? Har ni?
Frisnarken Vykort Glace

WHAT A WAY TO TRAVEL

DENMARK

About half the size of Scotland – mostly lowland – consists of islands.

COPENHAGEN is Denmark's only large port and industrial centre.

Places to note:
Harbour (Canal system) The City Hall
House where Hans Andersen lived The Little Mermaid
Christianberg Palace Round Tower Tivoli Gardens

Do you speak English?
Please Thank you How much?

Taler de Engelsk?
Vaer saagod Tak Muormeget?

Tivoli is not just an amusement park, with flowers, restaurants, music and all sorts of entertainment, Tivoli is also a symbol – a symbol of something charming and friendly, something happy and gay, that we cannot do without.

When Tivoli started in 1843, the gardens were laid out beyond the city's old ramparts. Today they lie in the heart of the city, surrounded by towering buildings that form an effective contrast to the picturesque pavilions amongst the trees.

Open-air concerts, the evening brings thousands of coloured lights to come on, culminating in a flashing display of fireworks in all the colours of the rainbow.

MY MEMORIES OF THE FIRST TRIP ABROAD

Going onto the ship and the things that happened on board.

The sugar container moving at least 8 ft from our end of the table to the other, as the ship bucked and rolled. All my fellow classmates feeling or being sick – I never did! One of the many scrimmages between dormitories, charging with a broom in one hand and a dustbin lid in the other; having my neck ricked out of joint; then I went above, where all this foreign money blew at me, and scampering around to pick up as much as possible. Yes, I did hand it to a teacher.

Getting ready for bed with fellow classmates, pyjamas on, socks and lights off, and the one guy snoring and everybody picking on him.

The countries: Norway – I remember buying the Norwegian flag and being told off for waving it when we entered Sweden. I remember my first cable car ride. Sweden – buying those little baby seals, one for my mum and one for me. Denmark – it has to be the Little Mermaid, who at the time either had her head missing or an arm, but I will be returning to Copenhagen later in the book with a totally different story to tell!

PS Thanks for everything, mum and dad.

SWITZERLAND

Wow, my second opportunity to travel happened while at secondary school. A trip by train right across Europe and into Switzerland. When the train arrived at Zurich, we were transferred onto a coach for a trip up the mountains to a skiing resort called Adelboden, a beautiful little village atmosphere, and snow everywhere, deep thick snow, it is so pretty and so white. Some of the little houses in the hills are so covered in snow they looked buried, so much so that people actually skied off of their roofs.

Our hotel was so picturesque, with little wooden shutters on the windows, the steep slanted roof, and the wooden beams inside and out.

Having never skied before, let alone even seen a pair of skis, I knew this trip would be a bag of laughs. Geoff and I shared a room. Our first day onto the slopes would be so memorable, after picking up our allocated skis and skiing boots which looked so big and clumsy.

We eventually got to the summit of the nursery hill, wearing our new ski goggles, mittens, bobble hats and waterproof sprayed skiing joggers, we were all set to go!

Well, when we should have been listening and practising moves, Geoff and I decided to push off, just to see how it would feel sliding over the snow. Perhaps we should have listened to the bit about how you slow down, even stop. Well, the assumption was if you do not like it or want to change direction just fall over, no problem, nice soft snow to fall on. Wrong!

That one push off seemed to last forever, we just seemed to gather speed, getting faster and faster, the thought of falling over, we were really moving by now, we both remained standing and kept going.

Unfortunately in front of us was a bridge no more than 10 ft wide which we were heading straight for, then miracle no. 1 happened. From out of nowhere our ski instructor flew past us, completed a complete U-turn and facing the both of us, stuck out two arms and took the two of us straight off of our skis, stopping us dead in our tracks and a good telling off to boot!

On another occasion Geoff and I decided to use our ski lift passes. With no skis we approached the lifts, got onto our chairs and away we went up the mountain side, fantastic view, people skiing down the slopes, people dropped all up the ski lift route, cameras, skis, gloves and hats.

Just as we approached the top of the lift, there were two men, one either side, undoing the chains which kept you in the chairs. We had no skis and no reason to get off, we had come for a free ride, and a view from the top. We had no intention of skiing and in any case we were not skilful enough! Well, as we approached the men started shouting at us in a foreign language. We pointed and indicated we were staying on, we wanted to go round and straight back down. At that point I was whacked around the head with a slap. The chain around my waist was wrenched open; I was pulled out of the chair and physically thrown into the snow outside the ski life building. Unbeknown to me, the same fate had happened to Geoff. I can remember walking around the building, crying. I saw Geoff coming my way and what a welcome sight it was. Now what do we do, stranded and no way down? We re-approached the ski lift. There was no problem getting down, you just took the chair, the problem being you could not stay on as the chairs went between a giant cog wheel which would have been extremely dangerous and definitely not allowed.

Our third encounter with danger could have been fatal. Our little group of about twelve in total had developed very quickly. After just a few days we thought we were brilliant skiers, we could turn, slow and even stop, so as an advanced group we were taken up high to give us a good long ski downwards, and off we went, falling at intervals, pulling others down with us. On one occasion we all had a good head of steam up, I can remember going down and one after the other also fell, skidding off in different directions but right near us within a short distance was a crevice, so deep that if you fell in I have no idea how anybody could get you out, and our whole section spun all around it. Only a yellow sign marked it with a black asterisk mark; another miraculous escape.

The evenings, once we got inside a local bar, there was also ice skating at an ice rink, there was also shopping. I bought mum a Swiss watch and a little temperature house where the man and woman come in and out. For me, a little Swiss pendant and a ski boot on a ski with matches in the boot. I still look at my black and white photographs in the snow, with my ski pointing skywards, and remember a wonderful time in the snow and recommend a skiing adventure to anybody.

PS Do not eat the yellow snow.

CAN YOU RIDE A TANDEM? YEAH, OF COURSE.

BUT AS FAR AS FRANCE, BELGIUM AND EVEN LUXEMBOURG?

This was the question my nineteen-year-old brother Bill asked me. Being fourteen and a keen cyclist I gave a straight answer – Yes. He asked, 'Do you fancy taking a tandem across the Channel and riding around bits of France and Belgium?'

Do I? Do I? Let's go! Let's go!

Preparation was in full force. Leather patches sewn on to our cut-down jeans for there are going to be many hours in the saddle! Also we had to join the Youth Hostel Association. With our heavy-duty rucksack attached to the back of the bike and a Union Jack draped and tied to the rucksack, we eventually pushed off. Bill at the helm with me at the rear – I do hope that he has not been eating beans!

We were heading for Dover, which was approximately a 100-mile ride. We were making excellent time and at Dartford the bike was loaded on to a special trailer and we got a free ride through. We passed a coachload of guys, which was parked in a lay-by, all with a glass of beer in their hands. One of them put his arm forward as we approached and I tried to take the glass. Unfortunately I hit it full on and, knocking it straight out of the guy's hand, the glass fell to the floor and smashed. OOPS, I apologise to that guy, as it was such a nice gesture. Just after that things started to go slightly wrong. The tyre started to rub on the frame and not long after that the back axle broke. Surely this was not the end of our adventure? We finished up sleeping the night in a bus shelter. Luckily Bill is not the type of person who gives up easily. His determination and engineering skills saved the day. We got the spindle required, upturned the bike and set about putting things right.

After our cruise across the Channel, open roads stretched before us all the way. I remember the roads being so straight, flat and miles long, sometimes it was easy for me to free wheel and allow Bill to do all the hard work.

Sometimes he put me in front and once I almost had a head-on crash with a French man coming in the opposite direction. After swerving all over the place we missed each other by inches.

Talk about strange looks sometimes. People would stop, stare and turn heads. Once we stopped for a drink of milk to discover people laughing and giggling in the shop.

The experience of Youth Hostelling was great and something to remember. We shared cooking and cleaning tasks, even making beds in the dormitory. Each hostel seemed to present different chores to carry out.

In Ostende, Belgium, we met and hung around with various travellers. I experienced my first cone of chips with mayonnaise poured all over them. And there was an occasion when a group of us left a restaurant without paying the bill. It was only once

WHAT A WAY TO TRAVEL

we had left that we realised and instead of returning we ran away laughing back towards the Youth Hostel. It was not so hilarious when the manager ran in after us. Needless to say , we paid the amount due with shameful bowed heads.

The route we chose took us from Calais along the coastline to Ostende then deep into Belgium itself to a beautiful place called Gent. It struck me as an old medieval town but the biggest buzz for me was when we reached Luxembourg. I remember seeing the Radio Tower with the words Radio Luxembourg blazoned on it in red letters and thinking of all those years listening to the station on my radio.

The trip was quite unique. When we returned to England and we were cycling towards home we picked up a puncture somewhere around Gillingham in Kent. By now the patches on our butts were worn through and there were now apparent holes in the cut- down jeans.

I do not know how or why we made the next decision, but we did. We pushed the tandem behind the local toilet and just left it there to rot or be found.

We then proceeded to hitch hike home. If I had my time again I would never have left that bike – even if I had to push it all the way home I would have made it. Such a sin to leave the bike, as we should still have it to this day. It had served us well and would probably have been worth a few bob now!

PS   Our Union Jack was stolen!

PARIS, FRANCE

A well-travelled American once said to me, 'Once you've seen one city you've seen them all.'

As time progressed I now know exactly what he meant. Although there are always exceptions to the rule and Paris has to be one of them. The others I will explain about later.

Eventually we ended up in the naughty part of town.

We had been drinking most of the evening and were a little tipsy when the youngest of the group stumbled across this beautiful lady. She was so slim, in these red skin-hugging pants, and a very well-developed girl up top. The young un was getting into a very passionate embrace, kissing, cuddling (probably French kissing). I must admit I was quite jealous, as she was a beautiful woman. We asked if she had any friends and she replied that she did, and suggested we followed her. As we stood outside this house she told us her friends were inside. This seemed a bit strange to us. She then told my young friend out of the blue that she was a man. I think all three of us said together, 'Pardon?' Without any further ado, my friend's hand was placed down below and he shouted that it was indeed a guy. 'He's a guy,' and took off running up the street and we were very close behind him.

I actually took a beautiful woman to France. I had won a trip from my work with all expenses paid. It was a trip to Paris for two. I had driven down. Now I have been flown down, what with an organised trip. We went to the famous Notre Dame and did all the usual jokes such as 'The bells, the bells,' and even the walk. We took the open boat ride down the River Seine and saw all the historic buildings, art galleries and generally took in the atmosphere of Paris. We watched the incredible roundabout at the bottom of the Champs Élysées with the traffic going every which way. We went up to the famous Arc de Triomphe, through the arch and thought of the Tour de France that actually takes this route. The Statue of Joan of Arc, thinking of what an incredible lady she must have been. All in all we took in the sights, sounds and smells of Paris.

Finally we stopped at the Champs Élysées for a meal. A waiter took our order then asked my lady friend if she would like any wine. 'Oh yes,' she replied, 'Do you have any German wine?' The waiter looked as though he had been smacked around the face with a wet fish. He totally ignored her question and walked off. She asked me what she had done wrong and I just explained that it is not the done thing to be in the capital of France with all their specialised wine regions and to ask for a German wine.

I return to France on many different occasions, one of which is a complete Tour de France, which I will cover later. Paris is a city I also return to on many occasions, sometimes passing straight through, or I would pick up different connections. But as you travel with me through this book, I have a travelling angel with me. My own guardian angel, but more of that later. Although in Paris I swear a miracle happened which I will also return to later on.

Paris is quite unique. I cannot quite explain about the romance of the city but I felt it to be a very romantic city to be in. Perhaps a great deal of that is down to Quasimodo and Esmeralda! Anyway, let's look at some of the sights, which cannot be missed. The Eiffel Tower must be the city's most famous monument and yet when seen from a distance you wish to be taller. Once closer and you look up at the engineering design and the vast metal structures it is appreciated just how unique the Eiffel Tower really is. You certainly feel compelled to venture up it.

Once at the top the view makes you feel as though you have seen all of Paris, which can be seen for miles. When I was there, I thought of the people who had thrown themselves off the monument, or the time when a parachutist jumped. It certainly looked a long way down and I was thankful of the safety nets to soften the fall.

I adore the words 'the Champs Élysées'. A place where you can stroll up and down forever. Where all walks of Parisians can be seen. It is like en masse, later afternoon/early evening, the locals mingled with the tourists, all just strolling around. Their 'fancy dress' can be seen, couples linking arms, patrons looking for a desired place to eat or simply having a beer or coffee, watching the world go by. This is probably the romance aspect of Paris, which is so difficult to explain.

My first trip to Paris was with a group of colleagues. A few of them had entered the Paris marathon and I joined them as their number one supporter. Thousands of men and women running, walking, stopping, all in the name of sport. I take my hat off to them. Our guys actually completed the course and received a medal, which I know most of them will cherish forever.

Once evening fell they could not muster the energy to go out, though three of us were game and decided to travel around the city by Metro. We were told that Paris is divided into four quarters and each had an individual atmosphere. We headed for food and entertainment presented by various street entertainers, from puppets to the white-faced clown. See page 236.

SPAIN

MAJORCA/ COSTA DEL SOL/ MALAGA/ TORREMOLINOS/ MARBELLA/ COSTA BRAVA/ BARCELONA/ COSTA BLANCA/ ALICANTE/ BENIDORM/ IBIZA/ SANTA EULALIA/ CALA LLONGA/ IBIZA TOWN/ FORMENTERA/ GRAN CANARIA/ TENERIFE

When I mentioned about Spain at the beginning of this book I was not having a go! You see, I spent over ten years going to Spain and the surrounding area. I have been to Spain on more occasions than any other place in the world. This must say a great deal about the place and its people. With each trip I hold fantastic memories, but it can become a trap. It is so comfortable there as the weather is good, the food is delicious, you are easily understood by the natives, it is inexpensive and not too far to travel. I would prefer to see tourists broaden their horizons and not to just lay on a beach each day but to get up, see the country they are visiting and look in on other people's lives.

Nevertheless I love Spain and have so many varied stories to tell, trips with single guys, couples, fiancée, wife, workmates and a whole group of guys.

In an attempt to offer you a flavour of each place I will relate a few stories to you.

Looking back I can remember days upon days of sun bathing,

getting burnt, looking and walking like a red crab, frantically applying sun lotions, creams, aftersun balms to elevate the pain, drinking constantly, eating and endless card games whilst drinking duty free Tia Maria and cold chocolate milk. Also those fabulous nights called Bar-B Qs when we cooked sausages while drinking Sangria, wine, bubbly spirits, beer and liquor, wondering why my brain was feeling out of this world.

On one occasion it felt so bad that when I returned from the toilet I totally lost my bearings and instead of turning right to join the dance floor I proceeded straight ahead and right over a 4ft high wall, leaving my platform shoes high heel on the other side of the wall. I landed on the dance floor where I continued dancing with one heel missing.

I also carried out an amazing clay dish of at least 2ft in width and weighing an absolute ton, which I somehow got off of the wall and gave to our cleaning maid the next morning. She was surprised.

Hung over, we hit the beach. It was winter, with nobody around. We found a couple of deck chairs, sat in them and promptly fell asleep. At some point a Spaniard who was gibbering away asking for money awakes us. My first thoughts were that he had taken our photograph while we slept. As I stood to hand him some money, unknown to me, my leg was still asleep. I immediately fell to the ground, scrambled back up feeling dazed and gave the Spaniard money, while asking when the photograph would be developed as we were leaving the very same afternoon. He handed me a ticket and walked away, mumbling, 'Mad Englishman.' He obviously had not taken our photograph at all but just given us a ticket for the deck chairs!

My brother Steve came into his own on one of these occasions in Benidorm – the same drink mixture and he become another person. Normally a very thoughtful and quite shy person, he became the life and soul of the party, up on stage at every opportunity and being thrown off constantly. Eventually he won a big pink elephant and there is no way he had won. They gave it to him to get rid of him. I can remember trying to help him on to the coach to go home. Going up the coach stairs he took his hands off the rails and we fell out backwards on to the ground, just lying there laughing, with the courier insisting we behave ourselves, and get back on the coach. He swears it was me who fell out on to him, and perhaps it was!

The next day Steve had the squitters and had a little accident on his bed sheet. The offensive skid mark I told him to leave exposed for the maid to change. We went out and upon coming back I went straight to the toilet. Steve went straight to bed and, letting out a great big howl, he shouted, 'Yes, she's changed the sheet.' Then he laughed so loud and for so long. The maid had changed the sheets all right; she had turned it over and put it on my bed!

Staying with the squitters for my next story I, was also bad. So bad was the smell, Steve had to leave the room and go on to the balcony on one occasion. You know the saying, 'The bottom has fallen out of my world'? Well, the world had fallen out of my bottom! Just as I came out of the toilet there was a knock at the door. I opened the door to find a maintenance man standing there. He had come to fix the light in the bathroom. I was heading for the balcony to get some fresh air. The guy was in the bathroom for some fifteen minutes and that was as long as we laughed for. Boy, what a job he had, either he held his breath or had been eating garlic.

Once my friend Pete and the two ladies who accompanied us were climbing the steps outside the barbecue. Pete was behind me and kept pinching me between the legs and I would lurch forward and accidentally knock my partner who was in front of me. She warned me about doing it but it did not stop Pete from doing it again.

As I bumped her she turned and threw a glass of wine all over me. I was so stunned that I just reacted by doing the same back. Unfortunately she was a stunning lady, all in white. My wine was red and it also hit a group of Spaniards at the top of the stairs who raged on. We were lucky to escape with our lives!

The same lady was sitting outside when Peter asked her to dance. As he took her hand and pulled her to stand up, a glass came down from the roof above. It landed and smashed just where she had been sitting.

Probably all down to the demon drink. Well, too much of it!

Other silly happenings – sitting on the beach with my socks on because my feet were burnt so badly. Well, I have trouble with chapped lips, which I have to keep moist. I had forgotten my lipseal so asked the girls if they had anything that may help. I was offered a clear lipstick, which would cover and protect my lips and, of course, would not show any colour. I duly applied the lipstick all over my lips and the surrounding skin area. How the three of them did not laugh I will never know. The lipstick was bright red and I had smarmed it everywhere! They sent me across the main road to buy ice creams. By the time I had arrived back they were in fits of laughter and I was none the wiser until shown a mirror.

Carl and I (a workmate) took two weeks in Torremolinos. We had a blast. One night he entered the Mr Eulelia contest. He was asked to strip to the waist and flex his muscles. Being about 6' 5" in height and over 16 stone, he was a big lad. He drank gallons of beer, a one-armed contest, collected as many women's bras as possible. He managed to gather 16; the nearest to him was 4.

Then he was in the final, just the two of them. They had to pretend to swing through the jungle, call like Tarzan, swim across a swamp infested with crocodiles, then down two pints of beer. He had done it all like a star and won easily. I was so proud of him and everybody knew us after that.

Another great character-was Keith. He was never drunk, just always merry and so funny with it. Everybody loved him and laughed at and with him. I attempted to teach him to swim. Once he arrived on the two girls' lilos, I just laughed and laughed.

It was my thirtieth birthday and I was made up and dressed as a woman. We ended up at a disco in Ibiza town and the only way on to the dance floor was by entry down a slide. Pretty difficult with a long skirt on. We also had this old jeep we used to travel around in. Once we passed all the open cafés on a street full of German tourists. We had all bought old Spanish uniforms for a laugh. There were about six of us and the Germans started to jeer us and shouted. We all stood, laid a finger under our noses and our right arm straight out above our head and sang, 'Two World Wars And One World Up Do Da Do Da', then we cleared the hell out of there.

I found old Ibiza town beautiful, full of little white houses converted into tiny shops so picturesque and selling a range of clothes that were so bright, colourful and summery.

We went to a little island where we found everybody nude.

We also had a go at water-skiing. I got up first time, waved, fell in and never got up again. Also had a go at windsurfing. I could get up on the board all right and I could even pull the sail up. But I could not get it to move and if it did move, I fell in.

I have got a few more stories about Spain and its surrounding area. Again, later I will return with a different type of trip.

But I would like to leave you with one more story before I go on. It happened in Gran Canaria.

Julia and I were having a fab time; weather was fantastic so I decided to buy a white thong swimsuit.

I found one in a store and went to try it on in a cubicle. Once on, I wanted to show off so called Julia over. What with my tanned body and itsy bitsy trunks, Julia was holding back with laughter. The problem was the side strings seemed to be twisted. We tried in vain to correct them so I called the male assistant over. He pointed me back towards the cubicle and followed me inside. Once inside as I stood there, arms down by my side, his hand came round the front, dived into my trunks, coupling my wedding tackle in one hand. He shook them up, whilst twisting the side string at the same time. I was speechless as he left. I called Julia over and told her I felt I had just been manhandled, literally. He came back and Julia was howling with laughter. I just nodded and said I will take them. He followed me back into the changing room, pulled my pants down and took the label out. I paid up and shot out of the shop like a bullet.

THE HONEYMOON AND STILL WANTED TO TRAVEL

BELGIUM/ GERMANY/ AUSTRIA/ ITALY/ VENICE/ MARINO/ SWITZERLAND

Normal ferry across the Channel, then an ongoing coach tour. We stopped along the route at many a different hotel. When we got deep into Germany around the Black Forest area, an area of hills and valleys covered in dense tree growth.

One particular stop we encountered two local Germans who introduced us to their language and local drinks and customs.

We spent about three hours in their company. Each party could not talk in one another's language so our communication was by pointing then by pronouncing the word. They would copy the sound, then repeat in their tongue, which we would echo back. For example: FLEGAR - FLY.

Well, they bought us drinks and we bought them drinks. They introduced us to Schnapps and how we should drink it. Straight up in the air and straight down. Even the older German guys were impressed of the amount and speed Pauline put them away. We thanked them for a wonderful evening, then they left.

That was when my first night was about to start. I was ready for my sleep. It had been a long day, added to that the drink, plus tomorrow we had an early start. But this was not to be a restful night. As soon as the Germany guys left Pauline became paralytic, she could not walk, talk or speak. How I got her up those stairs heaven only knows. She had lost all control in her legs and mind and, oh boy, was she about to be ill. She was sick everywhere and I felt so sorry for her. You know that noise that comes from deep in your stomach? Oh boy, I think she had emptied herself But she eventually fell asleep, so deep; it was like going into a coma. Next morning she just seemed to stare at things with a blank expression and no words.

The coach moved ever onwards, taking in the breathtaking sights of Austria. From high mountains to low valleys, snake winding roads upwards and down. All the way until we got to Innsbruck, a smashing town with lively activity and lovely friendly people. We visited the famous Golden Roof, an old tale that has stayed with me for life. You see, to all guides around the world, there are people listening and taking in what you are saying.

The tale is many years old. It is about two guys who approach the town folk and offer to build or restore this particular roof to be made of gold. The town folk love the idea, pay the two chaps a huge amount of money and wait for the outcome. The two guys keep the roof well covered for days on end. Eventually the roof is revealed to all, it is beautiful and shining in the daylight sun. Quite spectacular and everybody is so pleased. The men bid their fondest farewells, take their money and disappear. Bit by bit the roof starts to lose its gold. It begins to flake and goes dull. Under further inspection the roof appears only to be painted a gold colour. The town folk had been deceived, or so the story goes something like that!

WHAT A WAY TO TRAVEL

The evening entertainment was magnificent. It was a sort of bar/club like a beer cellar. I had my first Stein glass. It holds about 17/8 pints of beer. When it is empty just hold it up, it is collected and refilled. Did you know these serving ladies could carry four glasses in each hand? They were huge and so heavy, it took two hands to pick it up and pour into my mouth!

The entertainment started on stage, men and women dressed in their national costume. The women looked so pretty and the men so funny in their leather cut-down shorts with braces. Then the thigh slapping started, smacking hands and ducking, all to local folk music. You could not help but clap and tap along to it, twirling around, shouting and singing. It was brilliant to watch. Then logs appeared on stage and the men chopped and sang in tune to the rhythm and there is always one guy who gets everything wrong. Instead of ducking at the correct time, his timing was off and he would receive a slap to the face and a huge roar would go up from the crowd. I highly recommend a night like this. It really gives you a good flavour of the old ways and traditional Austrians.

We also viewed the famous tapestry of the fight between the Austrians and Italians. It is circular and captures the landscape and men fighting so well. It must have taken years to complete – so much detail you feel as though you're on the battleground itself.

Leaving Austria we enter Italy, heading for Lido di Jesolo. Here we would spend four days just relaxing in the sun after our hectic schedule. It was the first time I came across Italian food, maybe a soup starter, or pasta, followed by spaghetti, then maybe chicken and chips. Then ice cream or fruit to finish. We pigged out, to say the least. The beaches were great. Rows and rows of sun beds, all in a perfect line. This coastline is twelve miles of shops and cafés and the weather stayed hot and the sun shone.

On one of the many beautiful days on the beach, Pauline and I spotted a rock about 100 yards from the beach. We decided to swim to it to sunbathe from. We took a leisurely swim, stopping when we were tired. The tide was mostly out and being 6 ft tall I had no problem standing on the bottom. We reached the rock and spent about an hour on it, swimming around and having fun. We then decided to go back for lunch. The whole pattern of the sea around us had changed. The tide had been coming in and there seemed to be a wind up and an undercurrent we had not noticed on the way out.

I can remember it seemed like ages we were swimming and not really making any headway. Pauline was just behind me and seemed to be struggling and was extremely tired. I felt completely exhausted myself and I had a decision to make. To swim to Pauline and attempt to help her stay up or to swim like mad until I could reach a point where I could touch the bottom. Then I could encourage Pauline to swim to me. I was so tired I felt I might not have the strength to help Pauline and that we both may get into serious problems. So I swam towards the beach, dipping down, until eventually I could touch the seabed – a little further and I know I can stand. When I could eventually stand on tiptoes, I shouted to Pauline that I was standing and asked her for every last effort to reach me, shouting and encouraging her. Eventually I pulled her in towards me, she was exhausted. Slowly I bounced up and down and got us nearer and nearer to the shore until she could stand. With our breath back we hugged and kissed, realising we had just had a very lucky escape. People; never ever take the sea for granted. She can always surprise you or catch you out.

Because we were the honeymooners in the group everybody got to know it and was so kind to us. We were showered with flowers, bottles of wine and bubbly, wherever we went. Pauline even entered a beauty competition and won. I was so proud of her.

There was one particular guy in the group, a retired police inspector, a huge guy with a big protruding stomach. He had loads of laughs and always a kind word to everyone. One day on the beach, he was sleeping in a deck chair. I had found a dead crab and crept slowly and silently behind him and dropped it on to his stomach. It slid down on to his swimming trunks, just as he was waking up. He threw it off of himself (I am sure thinking it was alive and about to pinch him). When he saw it was me who had done it, he gave chase. If he had of caught me then I am sure I would not be here today. As it was he stopped short and just roared with laughter. Thankfully!

VENICE

Venice is everything you think it should be and more. It is a magical, mysterious place; the waterways make it totally unique. Standing in St Mark's Square makes you appreciate the whole view and atmosphere of Venice. The old church steeped in history, the famous little bell, the Rialto Bridge and the stories that go with the views.

Plus hundreds of pigeons flying and settling everywhere and, of course, you must take a gondola ride down the Grand Canal. It is so picturesque and colourful. You find yourself taking one photo snap after another.

Also, go down the backstreets as they have a totally different look and atmosphere to the main square. There are also beautiful restaurants with good food.

A trip to the island of Morano is a must. You can view the molten glass furnaces and watch the skills of the glassmen and blowers. They can put so much colour into their creations. I purchased a beautiful clear glass horse with a red streak running through it. It is so delicate with fine craftsmanship.

ROME

I mentioned earlier that the city of Paris was one of the exceptions to the rule. Well, to me, Rome must be amongst one of the greatest. Its history is there for everyone to see, its beauty and architecture can be touched and it's a thriving city with past and present hand in hand. To me it's got everything that a visit to Rome must be – a must in anybody's lifetime.

As you go round the city think of the power of the Roman Empire. Think of names like Julius Caesar, Nero, Michelangelo and many Popes who have trodden this hallowed grounds and you will start to realise what a special place this really is. Just take in the sights that one city holds.

The Colosseum: you can see this as an ancient site. To think about what the shell that is left used to be like when whole, with each empty space filled with colourful marble. The inside once had a floor and below the tunnels can be prison cells. The seats, which look like steps, where so many important and notorious guests have sat over the years. This is like stepping back in time.

Other places of interest, the Roman Forum, the magnificent Spanish Steps which we walked up and down, which at the time had flowers either side, the Piazza Venezia, the Monument to the Unknown Soldier, then by way of the Circus Maximus you can reach the top of the Janiculum Hill to enjoy a full view of Rome and its seven hills.

There are beautiful statues everywhere and water fountains like the Piazza Navona, or beautiful black lions laying at the foot or entrance to monuments. The stories of Hercules and Roman gods. I purchased a statue of one of Hercules' tasks; it is of two nude men wrestling together.

You can stand in St Peter's Square and be in awe of the structure, statues and the famous church and if you are really lucky, like we were, you will see the Pope emerge on to the balcony. Or you can go through the huge black doors into the church and view the magnificent paintings and sculptures, or even touch the Black Lady statue that has been touched so much her foot is like a stump and so smooth where it has been touched by so many over the years.

Or you can visit the many art galleries and museums with all their glamour and treasures inside. Or the famous Sistine Chapel with the painting of the chapel on the ceiling where the two pointed fingers do not actually touch although look as though they do.

WHAT A WAY TO TRAVEL

Rome over the years has been rebuilt upon itself. In the outer parts of town the evidence lies at the bottom of the buildings. You can actually see different layers of building materials laid upon each other. Dating right back to BC, when you touch it, it just crumbles in your hand. I am sorry, Rome, and I know people should not do it, but the piece that fell off into my hands I had to have, and brought it home. I had to have something dated before BC. It now sits in a replica of the Colosseum on my display cabinet.

Then there is the Trevi Fountain. Well, we took the usual photographs posing in front of the fountain, and then we remembered the old saying, 'If you throw a coin into the fountain over your left shoulder, it would mean you will return to Rome one day.' Panic, I had no coin, I had to improvise and all I had was an old used flashcube from the camera. So we set the photo shoot up and I would say 1, 2, 3, raise my left arm and throw the cube in, Pauline would take the snap. It worked perfectly but would the request work for me one day to return to Rome? I so much wanted to.

As the coach pulled out of Rome, the whole group started to sing spontaneously, 'Arrivederci Roma, for now's the time to go.' A tear rolled down my cheek, I felt quite touched and choked!

PS The magic flashcube did work, as I would be returning to Rome again.

FLORENCE

We arrived in Florence, the city of the greatest architectural forms and works of art and sculpture known to man.

WHAT A WAY TO TRAVEL

Ghiberti's Gold Doors are unique in their exquisite beauty and craftsmanship. The Ponte Vecchio, lined with gold and silversmiths, is a riot of life and colour. I think if you are an arty type person, this probably is the place for you.

We left Italy, reaching Lake Geneva in Switzerland, also up through Germany, especially the vineyard country, taking in a beautiful boat trip in the evening down the Rhine, and eventually heading for home.

This was a superb trip, a great way of seeing a great many countries in a short period of time, plus the friendships you form on the coach with the people you travel with – also it was a honeymoon!

I did do a separate trip to Italy, mainly a beach holiday to Rimini and Cattolica on Italy's Adriatic Riveria.

Again I return to Italy for a different type of holiday experience which I cover later. But the start of this next holiday adventure began in Venice. It was a cruise around the Mediterranean. Do you know, I enjoyed my second visit to the city as much as my first?

CRUISING THE MEDITERRANEAN

ITALY - VENICE/YUGOSLAVIA - DUBROVNIK/
GREECE - ATHENS - MYKONOS - RHODES -
SANTORINI - DELPH/TURKEY - KUSADASI - EPHESUS/
CYPRUS/ISRAEL - JERUSALEM - BETHLEHEM/
EGYPT - CAIRO – GIZA

After leaving Venice on our incredible cruise ship, we were heading for the fantastic town of Dubrovnik in Yugoslavia. This town is totally enclosed within its own walled defence, even entry is gained through a medieval archway. Once inside it is unbelievable, with its cobbled streets housing structure on the hillside, its magnificent squares and the beautiful quaint shops. It is all there within the walls and as you walk around looking up at the old structures you cannot help but think back to ancient times and, as the years have rolled by, very little change has taken place. With my luck, as I was there, music filled the air and marching bands and people with their national dress appeared from all of the different streets and made for the main square, carrying banners and flags from their own local regions. It gave the visit a unique carnival atmosphere with additional sights and sounds.

The shopping is so wonderful. The tiny shops and friendly people can hold your attention for hours just by looking at their art, crafts, and workmanship. When I heard of the recent problems in Yugoslavia when they were bombing Dubrovnik I felt a sense of sadness. Not only for the people but also for the beautiful buildings and history being destroyed and, of course, temporarily taking away the opportunity for others to share this quite unique and beautiful place.

The beauty of cruising is, after a great visit on land, it is 'up anchor' and while you are travelling to your next destination you can relax, enjoy yourself, mingle, have fun, take in what you have achieved that day and what you hope to achieve at the next port of call. No organising transport, hotels, the food is all there, all you have to do is select what you require and, believe me, there is plenty of it.

GREECE - ATHENS

It is amazing! You go to sleep after leaving one port and awake to enjoy a totally different environment and another new experience and, oh boy, this one was going to be extra special. You see, it goes back to when I was a young teenager. In one of our history lessons, the class was asked to draw the Parthenon in Athens. I got the library books out and began to get so involved in sketching the ancient monument and reading up about the place. I knew deep down in my body that one day I would stand alongside the Parthenon, and even touch it! And today would be that day.

The Acropolis was everything I thought it would be. It stands high on a hill, and it can be viewed from a distance, but when we arrived by coach it parked right opposite the main entrance under the shadow of the hill, so the first thrill was to climb the hill and, when you reach the top, there it stands in all its former glory. Standing bold and erect, surviving the span of time. You feel beams of delight come across your face; my eyes were probably bulging as well. I certainly could not contain my smile. I hurriedly approached the monument and touched the sacred structure and thought back to when I was a child. I knew then, as I knew at that moment, this was meant to be. I was meant to be here. Another stroke of fortune was meeting a fellow traveller on board ship - an American who was a scholar and extremely knowledgeable about Greek ways, both past and present. Especially about the Greek gods and history of the Acropolis, plus he had a brilliant way of delivering stories which made them fascinating and compelling to listen to. Also, you could ask any question and he seemed to know the answers. He became my personal guide and explained about Zeus, Athena, the temples, and of course the famous story of Pheidippides who had run from Marathon with news to the Acropolis to deliver his news, then die, and hence how the distance and race are known as the Marathon today, because of that run.

Also the night show is a must. You sit on an opposite hill and the story of Greece and the Acropolis is told to you via voices and lights, even to the point where red lights completely light up the evening sky. Glowing, they show how once the Acropolis was completely ablaze. It is so effective and leaves you with an everlasting memory.

We also took a trip to Mount Olympus where the first Olympic Games were held and where even today the Olympic flame is caught alight using mirrors from the sun's rays onto the torch. The arena is still intact, the running course and the old ruins, and you can cast your mind back to the days when men were naked and competed against each other. It is now known as sport and I do not think even the early Greeks would think it could be so international at this present day after their humble beginnings.

As the ship sailed on and around Greece it stopped just off Mykonos. This is a beautiful island, sun-kissed with all the buildings ultra white. It is an incredible little fishing village, in a tiny bay with fantastic small windmills, lots of minute fishing boats with pots and nets on the quayside. The locals, hardened fishermen, sit outside the taverns and simply watch the world go by. You can walk up and down the little alleyways between the whitewashed walls. This would be a smashing place for a holiday and oh, by the way, on the other side of the islands is a nudist beach which is extremely popular, or so I have been told!

Other small islands we visited were Santorini, with such a magnificent view from the hill top, Delphi, steeped in its history and ancient ruins and Rhodes, which was the home of one of the Wonders of the World - the Statue of Colossus. There are two pillars left to indicate where the feet of the statue straddled the harbour entrance. If you look up reference books on the old ancient wonders you can appreciate what these structures must have looked like and why they were called 'Wonders'.

The excitement on this cruise just seems to build and build; not only has everything we have seen so far been fantastic but what was to come was to be breathtaking.

ISRAEL

As we sailed into Haifa, I could not help but think of the words 'The Promised Land'. I had always promised myself a trip to Jerusalem. Do you remember being a child and maybe introduced to God and Jesus, the little picture books giving you an image of our Lord the Saviour? As you travel along the road getting nearer to Jerusalem, these images start to come back to you. The crucifixion, the cross, Jesus carrying the cross to the hill, the resurrection, the followers, the last supper, the miracles performed and, believe me, being here is like seeing a miracle all around you.

Old Jerusalem with its golden domes, the churches, shopping bazaars, the town is marked with stopping stages marking Christ's path tracing his last footsteps. On my visit, as luck would have it, a group of people were retracing Christ's footsteps and the leading man was carrying a heavy cross across his shoulders. The stump of the cross was dragging behind him, the group following were scattering flower petals and singing. It made me feel as though the past was happening before my very own eyes.

Then you enter the sacred church and go to the first level. There are incredible stained glass windows and, what with the colour in them and the sun shining through, and the cross with a replica of Christ, you actually feel as though the beam of light comes direct from heaven.

This is where, we were told, Christ was crucified, although a priest tending candles informed the couriers not to tell people this.

No one can take away the image I had created in my own mind.

WHAT A WAY TO TRAVEL

To me, I could see the hill where Christ was crucified flanked by the two thieves. To me, I could see Christ in all His glory with the crown of thorns and his arms outstretched. Do you know, I felt so humble and extremely honoured just to be here?

Below you can actually touch the tomb of Christ. There is a little hole that you kneel down and put your hand through. On the floor is a small basket with tiny wooden crosses, which you can take for a small donation.

This was a totally unique experience I will never forget, and yet there is more to come.

After strolling through the narrow shopping alleys, I saw an ornament I knew I had to have. It is a wooden carving of Christ carrying the cross, and I knew when I got it home I would be able to look at it and rekindle the wonderful memories of this momentous visit.

I went inside the shop, being a salesman by trade, and knowing that bartering over prices is a way of life in some countries, I decided to put on a show. I began by saying my Jewish friend in London called Doron told me to come to this shop, as I would get a very good personal discount. I think the owner was so confused by my opening statement he acted as though he knew Doron, when there was no way in the world he did. We soon swapped prices and agreed on a price very quickly. I only paid the equivalent of about £50 and yet its value to me is priceless. The shopkeeper even told me he enjoyed this particular sale!

I carried on browsing the sights and taking in the smells and sounds, touching places with names known the world over:

WHAT A WAY TO TRAVEL

The Golden Gate, Dome of the Rock, Mt Zion, the Garden of Gethsemane.

Eventually coming across the Wailing Wall, there were so many people at the wall, praying and placing their written messages on paper into the wall. To the left was a cave opening.

I could not resist and had to venture in. I was so impressed by their prayers and commitment. Some people were kneeling and rocking to and fro. Out of respect, I did not stay long or stare, but to have been part of it and to share that moment just filled me with wonderment.

But it just keeps getting better because our next stop was Bethlehem, and a visit to the Church of the Nativity. The birthplace of baby Jesus Christ. I did not expect a stable and a crib to survive the ages. I just did not realise the area would be within a church surrounding but, walking inside the door, I was physically shaking with excitement and anticipation as we walked down the small, worn-out steps down towards the area of the manger.

Born of the Virgin Mary, the 'Star of Bethlehem" in the grotto of the Church of the Nativity marks the traditional place of Jesus' birth.

The angel said, 'Today in the city of David a deliverer has been born to you, the Messiah, the word. And this is your sign: you will find a baby lying all wrapped up, in a manger.' (Luke 23 10-12).

And as I stepped outside I looked to the fields and thought of the shepherds down the road. I thought of the three wise men and gifts they were carrying - gold, frankincense and myrrh, then I looked to the sky and thought of the bright shining star.

And as I looked back at the church I though of Joseph, Mary and their new baby Jesus and of the Archangel, the little donkey and cows all in the stable. And in my head, the Christmas carol: 'Away in a manger, no crib for a bed, the little Lord Jesus laid down his sweet head'.

Also I thought of: 'Oh little town of Bethlehem, how still we see thee lie'. At this moment I realised just how moved I was by the whole experience. So I went to a gift shop and purchased the Star of Bethlehem, one for me, and one for mum and dad. Then I captured all my memories and put them into the star. Now all I have to do is hold the star and they come flooding back. At home placed in the circular star is the little wooden cross.

EGYPT

As the ship was heading for the port of Alexandria, a report came through informing the ship in front of us that the Achille Lauro had been taken over by terrorists and people had sadly been killed. Also a report that Americans had been stoned on land. The Captain was extremely apologetic but had made the decision not to sail into Alexandria. Imagine, I had come all this way to be denied the visit I wanted so very badly. Was I being greedy, perhaps I should be satisfied with what I had? A determination came over me, I will go, and I must go! I discussed my plans with my fellow travellers at the dinner table. Jim, an American, decided to accompany me although his wife was not too pleased. Especially as it was their anniversary while he would be away.

But go we did! The plan was to fly down to Cairo, using airline El Al. After we had checked in, we experienced an amazing security check. Everything was pulled out and checked to the extent even our toothpaste was investigated. Because of the problems in the particular area, the tension was added to on the flight, which had to fly over Israel's territory and, at the last minute, turn over Egyptian territory.

Cairo airport – people were milling everywhere. It was very busy and there were long queues for everything, including passport control. When we arrived we needed to pay our entry stamps which are stuck to your passport. We queued then I was informed mine would cost £120 while Jim's would be just £20! This would almost wipe me out but, as I was here, I supposed I would just have to pay up!

I have not told you about my guardian travelling angel but the story I am about to tell will show of the early proof I have. With so many people in that area, so many needing help and we were lost, out of our depth, nowhere to stay, no travel plans, no idea what to do next and we still had to face those queues. I turned to an Egyptian guy, proceeding to tell him about how much the guy behind the counter wanted. He just simply said, 'Follow me,' and I did. He went straight to the counter and a great deal of shouting took place. He then told me to give the man £12 for me and £4 for Jim and our passports.

The official snatched the money, stuck down the stamps while mumbling and moaning, then threw the passports back to us.

'Follow me,' the man said. There were four queues with well over 100 in each line. He took us straight to the front, got the stamp on our passport and moved us into customs, waving and talking to the customs officials. We passed straight through. Jim said, 'Why do I have this feeling this is going to cost us money?' I smiled and, when in Rome do as the Romans, Jim said, 'That's what's worrying me, this is Cairo.'

The man stopped, shook our hands, bid us farewell and told us to have a good journey. Jim and I looked at each other. 'Do you have a hotel to go to?' 'No,' we replied. He answered, 'If you turn left just here, there's an agent who can help you at very reasonable prices. Give him my name,' (which he wrote down). 'He will give you a very favourable discount.' We thanked him again and sort of hinted, did he want a tip? No, no, all part of the service!

What a nice guy – without his help what would we have done, and all for nothing, done just out of kindness?

We turned the corner and headed for the closed shutter of the recommended agent. It looked closed, completely empty.

So I gave it a bang with my fist, the shutters flew up and I received the shock of my life. It was he, the guy who had just helped us. We roared with laughter, I just could not believe it and I certainly did not expect him to be there. At that moment in time I think he could have sold me anything.

And he was fair to us, starting with budget; this would dictate the conversation, like grade of hotel, and what we wanted to see. We listed everything we wanted, agreed a price and paid up. Now usually I do not just pay up front. Biggest rule of thumb, you will get ripped off later, and I think we needed to trust someone.

A taxi was laid on to take us to our hotel. They carried our bags to the door; an extended palm of the hand follows every

WHAT A WAY TO TRAVEL

movement. Downtown is quite a way from the airport and, do you know every driver drives with his hand permanently on the horn? It is just beep, beep, beep; even when nobody is around they beep. The hotel was ok. Well within our budget, but no three stars.

Morning started with wailing from the temples, a man calling out. It seemed to boom across the city. On the roof opposite it set the cockerel off, which in turn made the goat bleat. Oh boy, I am in Cairo and I am going to love it!

Well, we had our own personalised transit, but it was small and diddy. We picked up one other, a lady travelling independently, where we were going to none other than the museum to see the Treasures of Tutankhamun, the Boy King. And these are certainly treasures. The first thing that strikes you is the amount of articles on display – it is endless. There are the original photographs taken when the tomb was discovered and opened, the gold made into all sorts of ornaments, from rings to bracelets to necklaces to chains to fingernails. There is so much here – you have just got to go and see it!

There are solid gold boxes that fit within each other, at least six boxes, and I am talking six foot wide. It is amazing, one treasure after another, leading into the golden mask. This is a sight to be seen. It is absolutely fantastic to the most delicate detail. To the brilliant gold shining back at you, to the colour and, of course, the eyes that look right through you. Followed by the gold coffin, the king's magnificent throne, jewellery, alabaster lamps of quite exquisite beauty, golden statues, paintings, carvings, warriors with spears and animals, their incredible headgear, beads, wooden chariots, chairs and stools with so much detail. It is just unbelievable; all that history captured in one place under one roof.

What a brilliant start to the day but, oh boy, how can you top our next stop? The pyramids at Giza. Now remember, these are the only surviving wonder of the ancient world that you can still see and touch. They are fantastic, they are huge, and imagine how many people over the years have come to see them, from the most famous including kings and queens, world leaders to peasants, beggars, thieves, everyday folk and now me included.

I had to touch them, I had to climb on them, I even had to kiss them, but when I was told I could go right inside of them to the heart of the pyramid, to the burial chamber, actually was my whole body was blitzed.

A little old man was to be our guide. He looked well into his seventies; his whole body was hunched. I thought, 'Will he make it?' I am talking 150 yards upwards and the gap was no more 4 foot high in parts. But the excitement pushes you onwards and the higher you go the hotter it gets, as you are bent over and cannot stand upright, the sweat drips back on to you and the incline appears to get steeper, then you seem to burst into a room and you have arrived – you are inside The Great Pyramid.

The room had that very musty smell to it, there were carvings on the wall; it was sort of a cold room yet of course there was no air circulating. After all, this is a tomb.

We did not stay long; the old chap wanted his tips before descending. It was worthwhile, and what an achievement I felt, and I could now understand why our guide was sort of bent in shape!

It was good to get back out into the sunshine, fresh air, and to be able to stand upright again. As I looked upwards, I could see why it is called a 'wonder'.

As I was still thinking and trying to take in this great spectacle, I had a headpiece placed on to my head. 'Give me camera,' an Egyptian man was saying. In a state of shock I just gave it to him. 'Get on camel,' he instructed. 'I take photo.' The smile which came over me! I had always wanted to ride a camel – what a bonus.

As I climbed on the beast, I could smell him with his champing jaws and saliva dripping. He really is the ship of the desert. Up he bucked, backwards, then forwards. I felt like I was never going to stay on him. I grabbed his hump, and then he just swaggered off, wobbling me from side to side at a graceful, slow pace.

It was great, the chap snapping away with my camera. I felt like a sheikh of the desert, part of an Arabian night, as if I was Lawrence of Arabia, dashing with my headpiece.

It was another story trying to get my camera back as the Egyptian thought he was David Bailey. He even told me he was! Oh boy, he wanted every last penny out of me. I gave him tons, and why not? I had really enjoyed myself, and another first!

Our next call was the world-famous Sphinx. She lies so proud as though she is waiting to pounce, or as if she is protecting something. Her head is so aloft as though she is looking out to the desert, waiting for somebody. In front of her are her huge paws, which could swat any enemy. She truly is magnificent. You can take a photograph of her and have pyramids as a backdrop. These pieces together make it such a special place.

We had a wonderful driver/guide. He told us stories, pointed out things, possessed a good sense of humour and was extremely knowledgeable of all around us. He told us of how Napoleon was so jealous of the Sphinx's beauty that he fired a cannon ball straight at it, blowing her nose off. It is true, the nose is damaged.

We were taken to a local gift shop where we tried on local gowns. I purchased a replica Sphinx, a metal pyramid and a mummy-type statue, sort of made of bronze. We also visited a perfume factory, mainly the essence that you add to alcohol to make the perfume. Squashing the petals of flowers and collecting the liquid produces the essence. There were some incredible smells and fragrances.

I could not resist buying a small bottle of frankincense, as it would remind me of one of the gifts one of the wise men had carried. Lunch was taken; Jim had I think it is called 'chicken'. I passed; I was too excited to eat. What a brilliant day this had been.

But it was extremely hot, and in the afternoon we travelled deep into the desert. We also visited more burial sights which were underground, and were shown the symbols even those of Tutankhamun. We travelled along parts of the Nile and saw the locals at work and play, along with their places of living. We discussed the pyramids and how the structure was put together, and that at one time was completely covered by sand. I told the

WHAT A WAY TO TRAVEL

group my theory was that the pyramids were built downwards and not upwards, as it would have been easier to lower the stone blocks rather than to lift them upwards. We all discussed the day's events everybody had enjoyed so much. We have all been left with fantastic memories and just think all those people on the ship who had missed all of this. Mind you, Jim was not feeling too good – I think it was a mixture of excitement, fatigue and the chicken he consumed! We had one more call where papyrus grass is treated, beaten and stretched to be made to look like old paper. By the time they are cut, coloured and placed between two pieces of glass, they look so authentic. I had to buy two, one of the ancient Egyptians performing circumcisions on young adult males. They have terrific details, right down to the cutting tool, but it looks painful. The other one is my star sign, Leo, showing a very proud lion with reins being held by an Egyptian lady dressed all in white. Brilliant! Another treasure for my collection.

It was back to the hotel for a quick wash and something to eat. Our trip is not over yet. Tonight, as a special treat, we will be returning to the pyramids and Sphinx for a spectacular sound and light show. Poor Jim, he is not very well at all. He is so sick and tired and just wishes to sleep. I want to go to the show but I cannot leave him, but good old Jim insists that I go, but I have to promise to tell everything. No problem, I have just got to go.

Ah! This was fantastic; the evening night air was warm from the desert. It was pitch black; not a sound from the audience could be heard. Then a Richard Burton voice springs into action, breaking the silence. He told us to imagine back in time, to the great pharaohs, kings and the early Egyptian way of life. Then he informed us that we were standing where the greatest people on earth had once stood, past and present.

Cleopatra, Alexander the Great, and many more. And as he spoke and told us his story, incredible coloured lights came on and lit up the pyramids and the Sphinx. What with the lights constantly changing colour and dancing to music, a unique atmosphere was created. This was a brilliant show, the music got louder and louder while the lights danced everywhere. The darkness and silence were followed by a stupendous round of applause from the crowd.

By the time I got back, Jim was feeling better and I tried to re-create my experience but played it down a bit as I did not want to make Jim too jealous. By the time I laid my head down I was so shattered. What a day! A day I shall never forget. We were up early to catch our flight to Rhodes to join the ship. As we drove to the airport I can still hear those car hooters beeping away. By the time I got back on board ship I was ready for my shower, some good tucker and sleep. Little did I know that we had become celebrities because we were the only two on board who had made it to Egypt? Everybody wanted to know how good it was, but was it worthwhile? Yes, and I enjoyed telling everyone. Unfortunately, Jim's wife was not overimpressed. He had to do some grovelling and apologies for missing the anniversary but Jim, I am so glad you accompanied me. I needed it, and thanks, mate.

The cruise had not finished yet. Our next visit was to be the beautiful island of Cyprus. As you travel through the hills you are surrounded by orange and lemon trees. It seems a very quiet place with pleasant people. We observed the border with the Turkish side of the island and at the time our own military area with its housing and sports area. Most of the hills are covered in grapevines and the beaches look ideal just to relax on.

Today we are due to anchor off Kusadasi – Turkey. We took in the market area, which is full of sights and sounds and colour. It is great just wandering round looking at local crafts, but the reason was, here is a trip to Ephesus, an ancient civilisation town completely covered by the ground and only recently rediscovered. It is as though time stopped still, the place had been totally covered by soil. When it was rediscovered, everything was perfectly preserved right down to the paved streets, the old library, the bathing area, even down to their toilet system, which was holes cut into concrete slabs. In front of you runs a trough with free-flowing water, into which you would dip some kind of cleaning brush with which you would wipe.

They say they have discovered the first ever road sign. It is an instruction to turn left at the crossroads, indicated by a left foot with the big toe showing it to the left and a cross for the road. There is an old notice board with writing still on it. The chariots used to pull up outside to read what was going on in town. The chariot marks can still be seen in the road. A view of the entire area shows exactly how the town was laid out, including the amphitheatre. Everything seems just as it was and is so unique. It is said that disease wiped out the population and nobody visited the town, hence why it just got covered over. This is an amazing place to be in, I would recommend a visit to anyone, and this really is a discovery not to be missed.

Well, we visited our last port of call, next stop back home. But this has been an incredible journey with so much variation in the lands we had visited, so much history and ancient buildings, stories of gods and heroes, beautiful buildings past and present. This trip has everything plus the ship and all the new friends I had made on board, and the fact I came second in the table tennis competition – and that was outside with the ship rolling and the wind blowing. I have got some wonderful stories to tell and memories to hold.

HOLLAND - AMSTERDAM

And now a complete change of direction. My friend and I decided to take a long weekend break in Amsterdam, crossing by ferry and taking the coach all the way there. Upon arrival at the hotel we were told that the hotel was overbooked. They did have a room for us – ok, but one of the beds is a 'put-you-up'. Well, Mick booked the hotel, surely he should take the 'put-you-up'? A friendly argument broke out but we were both very strong-minded. The only way to decide was a game of Spoof. You both have three coins and you can put from one to three in your hand. The other person does the same and you then take turns in guessing first how many the two totals are. Mick had never played before but roared into a 2–0 lead. Luckily I got the last three hands right and claimed the bed!

After perusing the centre, taking in the local surroundings and getting used to our bearings we decided on a riverboat cruise. A glass top boat that would give you good vision all around. The whole place is a maze of waterways and canals. To think that so much land has been re-claimed from the sea, it is quite an accomplishment. The houses rising above are very colourful and each has its own personality. We were told that in the olden days tax was levied against your house depending on the width of your property and not the height, hence they were built narrow but high. So narrow that many homes have hoists to take furniture up because the width presented a problem. We actually managed to see the smallest width house. If you stretch both arms out you can touch either wall.

There are many bridges along the waterways but as we looked back at one particular bridge at the bottom a waxworks of a man – a prisoner – stands looking back. The place used to be a prison, which I imagine must have been extremely damp and cold.

We certainly enjoyed our riverboat trip. It is a great way in which to get around and see everything. We decided to stop for food at a wafelen and were served up something which resembled a pancake. Hot pastry with a banana filling coated in icing sugar accompanied by fresh fruit and three different flavoured ice creams. The taste was absolutely fantastic, a mixture both hot and cold, bitter and sweet. Each mouthful twanged a different taste bug, absolutely superb.

For the afternoon we decided on a trip to the flower gardens of Keukenhof Just outside the gardens the coach stopped at a garden centre. As everybody knows, Holland does have its fair share of windmills which are scattered everywhere. Well, at the garden centre we had a chance of our photograph being taken next to one. A miniature version of one was made, also giant dolls in traditional national costumes. And if you wished to order flower seeds to be sent back home, this was no problem.

Then we entered into the gardens, which were so picturesque. There were flower fields everywhere. All shapes and sizes, every colour combination under the rainbow. It was just so beautiful, rows and rows of tulips, hence the song 'Tulips from Amsterdam'. Deep, thick green grass broken by flowerbed after flowerbed. In the centre was a large lake with swans swimming.

There were greenhouses full of flowers, an eating area for picnickers and the flowers mingled with trees. The flower beds were cut into all types of shapes, some a sea of blue broken by circles of red, yellow, orange, gold, pink, any colour you can imagine.

And the incredible aroma from the whole area, the air smelt sweet.

Nighttime takes on a new slant. We decided to take a beer in a local bar where we were offered all types of dope to smoke quite openly. It is legal in Amsterdam and you can literally choose whatever takes your desire and just light up.

We walked around the red light district, all the shops with their products openly displayed, books, gadgets, you name it.

You can also see the ladies of the night showing their bodies. You can stand outside a window and watch them put on an act to entice you inside. Again, it is totally legal over here. (Mick has his own story to tell!)

Also the city changes at night. Lots of beautiful lights change the look of the city. You will get approached by people willing and able to sell you anything that you may or may not need.

Well, the following day we took the tram around, walked down the little side streets and we stumbled across a famous clog. Yellow in colour and it was huge, shaped into a boat. I could not resist a photograph, also an old bike converted into a barrow bike.

WHAT A WAY TO TRAVEL

So if you ever want to buy seed flowers, cheese, clogs, dope, diamonds or even sex, this really is the place for you. I settled for a little china clog and windmill. All in all this was a fun weekend and again, well worth doing. The people are very open and friendly, absolutely no problem with the language barrier.

GRAND TOUR OF FRANCE

Well, it all starts at Ramsgate. The place of my birth. We caught the Sally Line to Dunkirk. My brother Steve and his wife Pauline had hired a car from the French side to make sure we had a left-hand drive car. It is so much easier to drive and safer, too.

Although our first stop was Dunkirk I wish to cover this area at the end of our story as we do return to Dunkirk.

The first day we felt good but unfortunately it was raining so we pushed on down to Rouen, passing Abbeville and eventually reaching Caen, where we stayed the night in a bed and breakfast. It is great practising the small French language I know, but it gets us through.

Breakfast we had our first hard roll and jam which we have to get used to. I also wanted my photo taken at the breakfast table with this beautiful French guest. She was so helpful and pretty, with a lovely English accent.

So we were heading for the Normandy beach landings of the Second World War. En route we come across the Pegasus Bridge, the first bridge to be liberated after the landings. Over the history of the battle that took place to gain the bridge I raised two fingers on each hand in the shape of the famous 'V' sign Winston Churchill made. Just alongside the bridge was one of the original tanks used in the war.

Then we headed for the beach landing area starting with, from right to left: Sword Beach/Juno/Gold/Omaha, Utah and in between is the American cemetery and monuments to the war effort.

On the landing beaches during the night of the 5th–6th June 1944, the Normandy landings started. Some 130,000 men and equipment were landed and some 10,000 men were killed on the first day alone. If you try to take this all in it is so sad, what a great loss, but they had to succeed to free Europe.

The longest day, from the museums, military cemeteries, postcards you are given free and put together a picture of the time and day.

When you visit the cemetery they show maps of their success, rightly so, but behind are rows and rows of white crosses. This was the cost, success and loss went hand in glove. I have got a postcard of Winston Churchill smoking a cigar walking up the Normandy beach.

Brother Steve found a bullet in a bunker that was so old it probably came from the battle itself.

We pushed on down to Mont Saint Michel where we pitched tent. It is like viewing a castle on a hill totally covered. Then when the tide comes in it is totally surrounded by sea and at night it lights up. It is wonderful. Oh boy, it was cold during the night and come morning we put the tent away, never to be used again. There is no need to in France because they charge you per room and not per person, so with three to a room it became cheaper.

We pushed on down through Rennes, Nantes, down to La Rochelle, taking in the beautiful and peaceful countryside, eating fresh bread sticks, cheese and fruit, alongside the grape vines we would picnic.

We pushed right on down to Cognac country, Bordeaux and its wine region and when we could we visited the distilleries, tasting the products and purchasing little souvenirs such as a small bottle of Cognac, a bottle of Château Brugier '86. We used to drive the days at an easy pace, stopping when we wanted to, then get a room for the night, have food, local drinks, lots of laughs and plan our next day.

One time we stopped at a service station for a toilet break. Now, if you have been to France then you will know that not all toilets have seats. This place was no exception; you had to straddle a hole in the floor and either stand or squat. Now, I had gone into one and Steve into another. I finished quickly, deciding to wait. Steve, however, took longer. I shouted to him to throw the toilet roll over the top, telling him I was on the left whereas, in fact, a chap occupied it. I can imagine this man squatting then all of a sudden this toilet roll comes hurtling over. Steve was none the wiser.

We pushed on down to the harbour port of Marseilles. It is picturesque with the little boats moored. High on the hill above the harbour is a castle. When the night falls with all the lights on it is really relaxing, with a good meal and a bottle of Burgundy.

Now we were off to St Tropez, playground for the rich and famous and, of course, us. I love this type of place, beautiful beaches, loads of restaurants, all types of watersports. In the evening you dress up and walk around, posing. You have got to be seen to be in and you have got to be noticed. These are what

I call the beautiful people, the sun was hot, hot, hot, and we hit the beach. You do not need swimwear here, some were topless and some were bottomless as well. But it is a great name and a great place to visit.

We drove right along the coastline of the French Riviera, the Côte d'Azur. There are so many places to stop, little towns, villages, sea fronts, little bays with wonderful soft sand. St Raphael, Cannes, Nice, Villefranche. We booked into a hotel at Théoule, which is about 10 km from Cannes. It was very reasonably priced, with a swimming pool and a hilltop view looking over the ocean. It was a great base to explore from and cheaper than if you stayed in Cannes or Nice, which can be extremely expensive. As we sat on the beach at Cannes we thought of the famous film festival and all the famous stars that had visited this area and here we were, in the same place. We purchased a can of Coca-Cola and pointed to it to remind us of Cans (Cannes).

It has a beautiful rugged coastline with wonderful topless women everywhere. I wore my white thong swimsuit and felt well at home. Mind you, in the evenings the mosquitoes did play up a little. They seem to adore me and I received many a nasty bite!

One of the evenings we travelled down to Monaco. This lives up to everything you imagine the place to be, and more. The signpost reads 'Principauté de Monaco' and it has incredible views of the harbour area and the palace that looks on the sea. We all got a real buzz out of being here. We had dressed up for the occasion, my one and only shirt, jacket and tie. You see, we

WHAT A WAY TO TRAVEL

were also going to the famous Monte Carlo casino.

As we stood outside the grand building of the casino taking our customary photographs we thought about the Formula One racing cars that zoom past this very spot. You could see the tyre marks. We thought of the famous names of the drivers who over the years had driven their cars over this very spot.

We entered the casino armed with a plastic beaker to carry our change and we hit the machines. Pauline and I had little wins, putting it all back. Steve, however, was much luckier and began to build steadily. We told him to get out quick before it all goes back. We tried our luck at the roulette table but it was not our night so we stopped, but it is just as fascinating watching others chancing their own luck just to strike a rich vein.

As the night drew in we got to a high point; looking below we could see lights on the palace, the road and the houses. It is a fantastic view and so beautiful. We had a wonderful time; on the way back we took a detour into the mountains. Coming down by car is breathtaking, the steep corners, the winding roads and the sheer drop made it an exciting ride home. I thought I was Stirling Moss!

After three fantastic days on the French Riveria it was time to move on. We were going back inland, heading for the Champagne country.

We travelled up through Avignon, Lyon, Dijon, Marne, and then right up into Reims.

When in Reims it is a must to visit the historic Champagne cellars. These are like underground cities and there are bottles upon bottles of lovely bubbly.

WHAT A WAY TO TRAVEL

The surrounding area is vineyard after vineyard, grape after grape and, of course, they always let you have a taste.

One of the visits was to the famous GH Mumm and co. Outside there is this huge magnum bottle standing next to it. It made me feel small – great photograph, though!

What more could you want being on holiday with good food, great company and a bottle of champagne to boot? It really cannot be bad.

Well, we are on the final leg of our journey, skirting Paris back up through Lille, then on to Dunkirk – our starting place, and where the car has to be returned.

The reason I wanted to leave Dunkirk until the end of my coverage is because this place is so important to me. It goes back to the Second World War and my dad was at Dunkirk. He was a regular soldier when war broke out and he was one of the first to leave for France.

On the evacuation from Dunkirk dad had told us he was on the last line of defence. He said that the Germans were getting nearer and the bombing heavy when he heard the order, 'Get the hell out of here.' Every man for himself, running for the beach and shedding his clothes as he ran. He entered the water and said after swimming about a half a mile out fatigue really set in. His comrades were dying and drowning around him. He swam on, all he could remember was he was on his last strokes, exhausted, when he was grabbed and pulled up on to a tiny vessel which took him to a larger ship. He said he only just made it, standing there on the beaches. I shed a tear for those men; our heroes, and I gave thanks to God that my dad had survived. Let's face it, if he had not then I would not have existed today.

Dunes and old bunkers cover the area but it has a kind of silent peace about it as well.

My memories of this trip; it was fun-filled with lots of instances and plenty of variation. There was the heavy rain at the start of the holiday, getting used to driving on the right, we used to have a dodgy windscreen squirter which when pushed down would squirt the people at bus stops or men on bikes we were overtaking at the time.

There was the different regions such as Brittany, Normandy, Bordeaux, Loire, Cognac, the Dordogne, Toulouse, the French Riveria, St Tropez, Cannes, Nice, Monaco, Monte Carlo, Provence and Rhone.

There were the monuments to the two Great Wars.

The Normandy landings 'D-Day', the fields of the Somme where my granddad fought and survived and Dunkirk where my own father had been and also survived.

There was a great château we visited where we were shown this incredible room. We jumped all over the bed, used the toilet, then decided not to stay because of the cost. Instead we stayed down the road in this flea-bitten room where we kept our clothes on to sleep and the toilet was outside! And instead of a meal at the château we had to be satisfied with soup in a run-down trucker's café, flies everywhere and food horrible.

We experienced the high-flying lifestyle of the rich and famous at St Tropez, Monaco and Monte Carlo.

We tasted all sorts of liqueurs and wines (red and white), brandies and, of course, champagne.

WHAT A WAY TO TRAVEL

One night after sinking a few too many, the three of us were sharing a room. Pauline got a bit amorous towards Steve. The lights were out and we were all trying to sleep when Pauline hurled herself at Steve. The momentum and force made them both tumble out of bed, Steve striking his head. What with all the commotion and laughter I turned the light on to see the two of them on the floor in hysterics and blood pouring from Steve's head.

We did have a good time with lots of laughs. We enjoyed the hospitality shown to us and the patience with our small knowledge of their language. By the end of this trip even Steve, who could not speak one word of French, could ask a waiter for three cups of tea with milk please in fluent French. I was impressed, but then he did have a good teacher! The funniest photograph; I told Steve to hold his hands up and I would arrest him with a plastic broken toy gun. Pauline would take the photograph. However, Steve would not put his hands up and said that he did not want to be a German. How I laughed!

AMERICA - USA

I think even the name sounds big and we have all heard of the American Dream. Well, my own dream was of America and, what with a name like Brandon, I felt I was going to find my roots.

Well, this might sound a bit flash but there is an element of luck attached. You see, I came across some gift vouchers which one travel agent in London would exchange for travel. They were worth about £600 so a friend and I, Eric, decided to book the QE2 to America, arriving in New York with a flight home included.

How could we resist? So the big day arrived. We had already travelled to Brighton the night before and stayed with Eric's family. The next leg of the journey was to Southampton, from where the ship sailed. What I did not know was we were taking a private plane and Eric was flying. At the time he was training for his pilot's licence and the instructor agreed to take us to Southampton. Knowing Eric as I did I could never see him as the pilot type, and he was so young. My heart was in my mouth as the plane took off, but I need not have worried as Eric was brilliant and so was the flight itself and the view. And what a way to arrive in style, in your own private plane – it cannot be bad!

WHAT A WAY TO TRAVEL

When you approach the ship and walk the famous gang plank that so many a famous person has done before you cannot help but look up at the splendour of this floating first-class hotel. The whiteness of the ship glares back at you, the large red funnel, and the dinky little survival boats. Actually, they are huge but in comparison to the QE2 they appear minuscule.

I was so excited I could not wait to get on board and explore everything, touch and sample the atmosphere. I wondered what my fellow travellers would be like, rich, important, kings, queens, who knows? But no matter what, I would be travelling the same way.

It is fantastic inside; everything sparkles, gleams and shines. The crew are so friendly and helpful. The cabins are either incredible or ok. Ours was ok. It was time to go outside as we were about to sail. I was not prepared for the view I was confronted with.

You see, it was the first sailing of the QE2 after refurbishment following the Falklands War. Everybody had streamers, a band played on the quayside, Eric's sister had come down and we were shouting furiously. It was a grand atmosphere, singing, cheering and shouting.

And then it sounded like a sonic boom as the QE2 funnels boomed out, black smoke followed and so did the champagne. We were sailing.

Leaving the harbour we were surrounded by a flotilla of small sailing vessels. It was so picturesque. This incredibly large cruise liner surrounded by white dots going every which way and balloons racing skywards.

WHAT A WAY TO TRAVEL

The trip was a five-day cruise and it is brilliant, all of it. From the food to the people and the entertainment. It was party time all the way. You could both relax and watch the water go by or you could swim, play games, eat, drink and chat. You soon get used to the routine of enormous breakfast, lunch, dinner and super afternoon tea and cakes. And the people you meet are great. Our table guests were brilliant and soon I looked forward to meal times. Just to catch up on what they had been doing and swapping your own stories. Even our waiters were fantastic and added to the fun.

It did not take long to meet and make a whole new bunch of friends and, of course, we had to put on our suits and ties to meet the Captain and have our photographs taken.

Some evenings we used to watch the sun set. When at sea looking out to nothing it is easy to feel small compared to the volume of water and another world under the waves taking place.

We decided as a group to stay up all night and watch the sunrise over Manhattan and the skyscrapers. As the sun broke through, what an experience. I remember the Statue of Liberty far in the distance, ever getting closer. Our group would split up and go its separate ways. As the sun rose and the picture of America awaited us I turned and had a romantic kiss with a beautiful young lady. This was a night and a morning I would never forget. As we got nearer we could hear the noise of the city awakening. The skyline ever larger and the bridges and shoreline getting closer. Then the fire ships coming to meet us, turning on their water cannons, spurting water so high. I thought of the last five days, I had a fantastic time. The best food and service, plenty of it and more if I so wanted, brilliant travelling companions, luxury, VIP treatment, the trip, the ship, the service, the people – all were 1st class. Well done, Cunard.

After passing through customs and immigration, this is New York, the BIG APPLE; we had a hotel already booked for one night. So let us grab a cab and head for it. Brilliant! The famous old yellow cab, always shown in the movies. We told the driver of the address and he advised us to lock our cab doors. This is because at traffic lights thieves tended to stick guns inside and steal bags. We replied, 'Pardon? Step on it', and he did. Oh boy, the speed in which we drove, how we missed the other traffic I will never know. We screeched to a halt, paid him and charged into the hotel. Once in the room we slept for 24 hours. What with no sleep the night before, the time difference and partying, fatigue, it had all taken its toll.

We awoke, switched the television on and for the first time ever enjoyed morning television. It had not arrived in the UK as yet. And the amount of channels blew our minds. It was time to eat and drink.

We discovered a lovely little café, and after ordering bacon, eggs and working out what 'easy over' was, or 'sunny side up', or types of coffee, we started to eat. Just then a beautiful lady appeared and she put her arms around the both of us and said, 'Hi, guys.' We thought, wow, they are friendly here but we are trying to eat. She asked, 'Do you need anything?' With a mouthful of food, I replied, 'No thanks.' Then the owner told her to get lost. We then realised we had been out only ten minutes and were propositioned. Well fed, it was time that we put together a game plan.

New York, this place is mega. You are in the shade because of the tall buildings and it has a unique noise. It is like a hum of activity, people busy going places, talking, chatting, and traffic noise, beeping of car horns, doors shutting. It has a buzz about the place and it is fast, alive with activity.

First things first. We had to check out of the hotel and move downtown to a cheaper hotel. Times Square, that sounds nice. Wrong, this is right in the middle of everything, and I mean everything. We managed to get a room, dark, dingy and cockroach-infested, plus ants as well. And, oh boy, the neighbours were something else. Noise, slamming of doors, shouting, yelling. Oh well, you certainly get what you pay for.

We hit the streets and we had so much to see. 'Hey man, wanna buy some coke?' we were asked as we stepped outside the hotel. 'No thanks,' I replied, 'We only drink Pepsi.' He laughed and told us to have a nice day, Muvver Trucker. I have no idea what he meant!

We were heading for what was at one time the highest building in the world, the Empire State Building. Just picture the image of King Kong, the blonde lady and the aeroplanes attacking. That's films for you.

To get there, we crossed roads that said, 'Don't Walk', security guards in shop doorways with guns. We even had blood pressure taken on the streets for a dollar. Mine was high, maybe it was the shock of being in New York, or was it the fear? No,

WHAT A WAY TO TRAVEL

definitely not, there is too much to enjoy to be scared.

The real way to capture this place is not by camera but by tape recorder. The sounds are unique, nowhere in the world is like New York.

We passed Grand Central Terminal and passed through Central Park. Once we had seen the Empire State Building we decided to go to an even taller building, the World Trade Centre, with its two towers.

We had to use the subway. At one time we just stood and watched trains coming and going. We admired the drawings and writings on each and every one of them. Inside was just like the movies, all types of characters on board and a little scary.

We stood under the World Trade Centre and took a photo looking upwards. You can nearly fall over just by looking up. Inside the lift goes up a zillion miles per hour. Zoom! Oh boy, does this travel fast; we changed lifts three times on the way up. You feel as though your stomach is at your feet.

But the view from the top is incredible. You can see for miles, the Statue of Liberty below, Ellis Island, the Bronx, Manhattan, Staten Island, and the tiny Empire State Building. Did I say tiny? Yes.

The water and the whole surrounding landscape is beautiful, the bridges, skyscrapers, downtown, uptown.

We decided to take the ferry, which travels a full circle around. On one of the banks, a group of boys dropped their pants and mooned. Everybody on the entire boat laughed. It is a great way of seeing everything and quickly, too.

Time to head back towards the centre. We had opted for

steaks tonight. Well, the steak was larger than the plate. It was so huge, thick and tender and only cost about £3.00. The waiter asked one guy how he wanted his steak cooked. He replied, 'Pull his horns out, wipe his arse and serve it.' Sitting there in the window and eating our steaks, we were able to watch the New Yorkers. We saw the ladies of the night, their pimps, arguments, tramps, down-and-outs, the police arresting a guy over the bonnet of a car, a fight, guys with music boxes at full blast and dancing on the sidewalks.

We headed for the lights of Broadway, shows, theatres, glamour and the glitz, hand in glove with the poor and needy.

We passed the cinemas showing all types of sex movies. We saw a film called 'Deep Throat' and neither of us understood it at all.

Well, it had been a great day, but like all big cities, about 11 o'clock at night it is time to get off of the streets and go inside where you will know you are safe.

Even at 7.30 in the morning our security guard insisted he accompanied us to the bus terminal. As you walk the streets you see the remnants of last night. People sleeping out, or passed out, people looking in bins and they stared in a cold and sort of envious manner.

Well, we are off. We are now flying to Buffalo, hiring a car, driving to Canada to see the Niagara Falls.

CANADA

The car was a beauty. A big, new, shining Yankee Doodle of a car, it was huge. Hop in, partner, let's head for the border. Canada, here we come.

WHAT A WAY TO TRAVEL

We, of course, took our photographs alongside the car, a 'Concord', holding our 'I love NY' stickers. We reached the border and stopped at the 'Stop for toll' sign. Above was inundated with flags. We went in and had our passports stamped and then were on our way.

Now, Niagara Falls has two sides to view from. The American side and the Canadian side. Following one set of signs we got a little lost and ended up on the American side, but it was all meant to be. You see, we stumbled across this guy who happened to be a pilot. After explaining to us where we had gone wrong and that not so many people came this side, he asked if we would like a helicopter ride over the Falls. 'You bet!' we chorused, but we said we could not afford it. 'Nonsense,' he replied, 'I'll do it for £10.00 for two. There's not much business around today.'

We nearly kissed him. Only £10.00. I had never been in a helicopter and certainly not over Niagara Falls. We ran to the helicopter, so excited. Wow, this is incredible luck.

Now, the thing about a helicopter is it goes straight up. I was so used to planes using a runway, then up; I was shocked just how quickly we were way up in the air. Still looking out front and forward I asked, 'Where are the Falls?' The answer came back, 'Right below ya, buddy.'

And there they were in all their splendour. A huge, vast amount of water flowing from every direction, forging and forcing itself together, then jettisoning itself in what looks like a hole in its natural defence wall, oozing itself forward, spurting forward and dropping itself onto a lower level.

What with the hum of helicopter and the roar of the water

below and the green mass of water turning into a white mist, this was truly an awesome moment.

By the time we had got back on the ground I was shaking just by the whole experience.

What a way in which to see the Falls, and I had shot a whole reel of film because it was just so breathtaking.

Our next move was to drive round the other side and experience the Falls from ground level. We booked into a hotel. Now remember, this is Honeymooners' Paradise. Our hotel had an indoor swimming pool, jacuzzi, sauna and a bed that vibrates.

We could not wait to get to the Falls. It was only a short walk alongside a small wall. You could easily see over. The mist from the Falls sprays you from some 200 yds away. It is great getting wet and feeling the spray on your face, and you can see the little tug boats going right up to the Falls and all on board wearing their orange sou'westers and getting soaked into the bargain.

You can get so near to the actual Fall that you can touch the water just as it is about to go over. And the roar of the water is incredible, the power it has and the journey it already has taken.

We did our usual poses for the camera with the Falls as a back drop, looking as though we were about to dive into the Falls but with so much mist we felt it would not do the cameras much good.

We took a little trip off the beaten track to go and see the Hydroplant where all that power of the water is turned into energy. Enough electricity is produced to cater for a very large area; there seemed to be hundreds of generators buzzing away. We found a little museum that told the history of the Falls and stats and figures, like how many gallons of water flow over, power generated and how men and women would go over the Falls in barrels and all manner of things. There is even old film footage you can wind by hand and watch them tumble over the Falls; some even died in the process. I thought, rather them than me!

As night fell, these incredible spotlights come on and lit up the whole Falls, then they would change colours like a musical display lighting up the water and making it glow in different ways.

This really is a wonderful place – it is unique and Mother Nature at her best, and would probably go on everybody's list as one of the new Wonders of the World.

Well, we headed back to the hotel, had a swim, jacuzzi and a meal including my first introduction to escargots (snails) and actually they were not bad at all.

Then after such an eventful day it was time for bed. Eric and I were sharing a bed; it helped to keep the cost down. Just lying there thinking about the day, what we had seen and enjoyed, all of a sudden I thought a bloody earthquake had erupted. The bed was bouncing around all over the place and so was I. You see, Eric had waited until I had dozed off, then slipped money into the machine and set the vibrating bed into action. We were both roaring with laughter. Actually, when it turned down a bit, it was quite relaxing and soothing. It must have been, because I did not wake up until the morning.

We were off again and flying down to Orlando in Florida. We drove back down and had a bit of time to spare before we had to take the hire car back. We had to go to a bank and ask about

WHAT A WAY TO TRAVEL

changing money. What I did not know was that the line I was in had a man standing behind me in the queue holding a gun. I was attended to and went to the back to the bank. Over there the counters only have a low piece of glass which would be easy to reach over. This is exactly what the guy did. He held the bank up and left. As he left the doors self-locked, alarms sounded and people were running and screaming. The police arrived and took statements. They were checking out that we were not an accomplice. When we gave our addresses they forgot us. I had not even seen the guy, but it was funny phoning the hire car company and explaining we were involved in a robbery and that we might be a little bit late.

Well, we flew out of there heading for the sun – Florida, the sunshine state. Arriving at the airport, having nowhere to stay we went to information. The lady behind the desk asked us where we would be visiting. We told her that a must would be Disneyworld. So she said, 'Why don't you stay there?' But the cost! 'No,' she replied, 'It's very reasonable, especially considering the built-in entertainment and no travelling to and fro costs.'

That was that. We booked into Mickey Mouse House! The Magic Kingdom, all your childhood memories in one place, your dreams, fantasies, illuminations, characters, things come to life here, Mickey and Minnie Mouse, Pluto, Snow White, Dopey, the list is endless. They all walk and move; they are alive and living in Disneyworld.

You can take rides you could only dream about, Space Mountain, pitch black, moving fast, being tipped every which

WHAT A WAY TO TRAVEL

way, lights zooming towards you, people screaming and yelling.

My first impressions, the heat, or more to the point, the humidity. The cleanliness, the colour, the organisation, with so many people coming and going. It is all so well organised.

Trains even pull up inside the hotel, an incredible hotel. The monorail that takes you right around the site. You can get anywhere and fast, the car parks with transport laid on to and fro.

The lake with all types of activity going on the water and off.

But the rides, or should I call them 'journeys', are out of this world. You can take a boat ride around a safari park with animals such as hippos, elephants etc., an old haunted house that goes to the basement followed by a sort of ghost ride train.

There are the pirates to see, the small world, and the glass bottom submarine. You can go into the future or back into the past. You can ride in a teacup on a saucer.

There is an old bus, basically there is everything you can think of and more. The best way of describing this place would be to say, 'You've got to see it for your own eyes.'

I do not think any words I use could do this place any justice. Not only is it full of daytime events but the evenings take on a new slant. You have a daytime parade of all the Disney characters and floats. But at night, lights take over. You had the electric light parade (which has now been replaced).

Well, we had four glorious days and nights; surely I will be coming back here. There is so much to Florida that I had not seen and I want to come back and see Disney World, especially when Epcot Centre opens later this year.

WHAT A WAY TO TRAVEL

Well, incredibly Eric and I met a pair of twins in Disney World. We exchanged addresses – they were 16 years old. That was it, little did I know they would have such an effect on my life. Looks like I will be returning here!

Well, we were skint, time to go home. This has been a fantastic introduction to America but there is much more to come.

We had enough money to get a Greyhound coach up to New York to catch our flight. The trip took two days; the highlight was passing the White House in Washington.

Unfortunately we only had enough money for two hamburgers, two Mars bars and two coffees but there was always water at every stop. We even asked a down-and-out, 'Buddy could you spare a dime?' But on the flight home we ate every scrap of the aeroplane food – delicious!

THE AMERICAN WEST

California, here I come. Right back where I started from. You guessed it.

We, Rosie and I flew into Los Angeles airport; this is an organised coach tour, all hotels and excursions booked in advance. Makes a change from going independently.

A fully escorted tour taking in Los Angeles, Disneyland, Palm Springs, Scottsdale, Oak Creek Canyon, Grand Canyon, Las Vegas, Yosemite National Park, Lake Tahoe, San Francisco and the Pacific coast, all aboard a fully air-conditioned coach.

LA even sounds good. Our hotel - the Hyatt, get this –on Sunset Boulevard. Rumour has it that Little Richie was staying in the penthouse suite. First thing, a guided tour of the city. We were driven right along Sunset Strip, 77 Sunset Strip, click, and click. Then around the homes of the rich and famous with their security gates and video cameras. Beverly Hills, you do not have to own a home here, just saying you have been is quite good enough.

On this whistle-stop tour we reached the Hollywood Bowl and were told this was the first place the Beatles ever performed at in America. Standing on that stage, just knowing the Fab Four had once stood there, was kind of special. Got to keep moving as we are on a tight schedule. Up to the famous Chinese Theatre to look at and touch the handprints of the stars who had made their indentation in the wet cement. You can actually touch and feel the exact same spot of these mega stars: names like Peter Sellers, Shirley Temple as a youngster, Burt Reynolds, Donald Duck, Sylvester Stallone and, of course, my favourite, Marilyn Monroe. As I placed my hands into the same formation of her hands I could not help but think how small and cute her hands must have been. Wow, it feels like you are actually touching them. There are these tiny shoe marks of the sole and heel and 'Gentlemen prefer blondes' etched into it. I had to have a photo of me next to that print.

Time to eat. Where else but Farmer's Market? You can walk around all the different stalls and select food from around the world. Well, after good tucker we are off to Universal Studios. This place is incredible. Not knowing just what to expect we were piled onto a sort of slow-moving train. As we chugged off I thought, 'Well, I cannot see very much.' Then we seemed to be entering a large type of hangar, going through these huge black doors into total darkness. All of a sudden red laser lights were fired at you, machines moved and rays seemed to bounce off of our transport vehicle. It was brilliant and a re-made set from Star Wars. The whole trip just gets better and better, to entering a bridge area that sort of collapses and King Kong roars up alongside you. You can see his huge teeth and there is always something going on in the background to also look at. You can observe how films are made, props, pretend fires that look so realistic, film sets, streets and houses, paintings and backdrops that look like real scenes.

WHAT A WAY TO TRAVEL

You can watch rivers part, flash floods, Jaws appearing out of the water about to gobble you up. You can watch a space walk, ride into a revolving ice cave. The whole trip is fantastic and comes highly recommended.

There is more to come in the surrounding area. There is a giant shark, stocks, visit to

TV and movie sets, see the 'A Team' stunts performed live. Thrill to Conan the Barbarian, a sword and > spectacular, see the Walton's Mountain, get your photo taken with King Kong, visit a Christmas Story, watch animals do tricks, see the famous Bates Motel from the film *Psycho*. There is a huge telephone, there is just so much to see, it is endless. You can even sit on the bike that gave ET a ride or you can be in Clark Gable's arm from the scene of 'Gone with the wind' by putting your own head through a hole and, to top it all off, on the way back to the hotel we saw a statue dedicated to John Wayne, and not to mention the famous Hollywood signpost up in the hillside.

Another day, another trip and this time to Disneyland. Now remember, this is the original and the first, which gives it an air of originality.

You will still see good old Mickey, Donald and Goofy, Pinocchio, and there are still the fantastic rides and Sleeping Beauty's' castle and that wonderful atmosphere which helps you feel like a small child, and there is always Tomorrow Land, Adventure Land, Fantasy Land, the Haunted Mansion and Frontierland, but most important of all it is called Disneyland and I feel so privileged to have visited Disneyworld and now Disneyland.

WHAT A WAY TO TRAVEL

This will be a whistle-stop tour but it is a great way of seeing a great deal of things, places and people in a short period of time.

We reach Palm Springs, one of the homes of Bob Hope and other celebrities and, oh boy, it is hot here – 90° in the shade. You need the air conditioning. At 10 o'clock in the outside jacuzzi drinking coke, listening to a group of guys talking about a visit to China sounds interesting!

Got us up at 6 am. Had a lovely swim in outdoor pool before breakfast and were on the road by 8 o'clock. We are off through the desert area, cowboy and Indian territory, of the days gone by. Stopped for lunch. Outside concrete seats too hot from the sun to sit on. Countryside, wild cactus, whirling sand and brushwood, the mountains in the background. Reached our hotel called Hotel Safari, sunbathed until 8 pm. It is hot, hot, hot. Time for a cool beer by the poolside.

Up early for another morning swim at 6 a.m. Heading down today through Phoenix, Arizona, beautiful windswept hills, deep Indian country. Down deep winding roads and valleys, up passes and over peaks, rich pine forests and flat plateaus, eventually reaching our destination. The Grand Canyon.

This has got to be a Wonder of the World, and a natural one at that. It is huge and goes on for miles and miles. It is so deep you can just about make out the tiny, twisting river below – the Colorado River, which is huge in reality but not from above here. Mind you, we had not just come to see it, we were about to fly around it. Mind you, we were told a week earlier that a helicopter and small plane had collided and everyone plummeted to their death. We were also told that it is dangerous because if

WHAT A WAY TO TRAVEL

you go down there is nowhere to land and soon you would not be able to fly so deep. What a challenge, what an opportunity, what an experience, what an idiot. Let's go!

Oh, it is breathtaking, the multiple of colours, the excitement. You only just miss the peaks and sometimes you feel as though you could reach out and touch the side walls, exhilarating, then a sort of sandstorm hit us. The wind got up and the rain came down. We began to buck and roll all over the place. We dipped, then pulled high. I have got to admit that I was scared shitless, so much so that this stranger (an elderly man) and I just clasped hands and squeezed each other tightly. By the way, we had never met. I took a reel of film but was praying we would return to the runway ASAP. If not sooner. What a relief when we had landed. It was a fantastic experience and I am glad that I had done it. Would I ever do it again? Definitely not. Would I recommend others to do it? Absolutely, yes. But do not ask me! Rosie consumed a great deal of chocolate before take-off, I had advised no, but you know women. She and other passengers chucked up on the runway. Rosie was first off of the plane, white and shaking, while I collected my certificate to say I had flown down and around the Grand Canyon.

Our hotel was a lovely old log wood cabin. But at 7.30 that evening we had to return to the canyon to watch the sun set on it. It was truly beautiful as the sun lowered. The canyon changed colours; it really was an incredible sight. A photograph was taken of Rosie and myself with the canyon behind us, capturing the setting sun. Fabulous.

What a perfect end to a perfect day. As I lay in bed that

night I thought of the Road Runner I had seen in the desert, the incredibly shaped cactus plants, Montezuma Castle where the early Indians from the 12th century lived in caves dug out of the hillside. Travelling through areas with names like Apache, Tonto, Happy Jack, Fort Apache, Navajo, Tombstone, Geronimo, Two Guns and Sun Valley. Going in and having a photograph taken outside a wigwam, seeing the Grand Canyon – a dream I had as a child, now fulfilled and loved. The colours and a rainbow appeared while we were there. The scariest flight of my life and watching that sun set on the canyon, wow, and I have got my precious certificate to prove it all.

Well, try and top that, no problem.

After leaving with our last sight of the Grand Canyon we pass and stop at William's Trappers County for bear furs, etc. Plus Kingman and Old Gold Rush Town. You can still pan for gold for a few dollars. It is probably still fool's gold! But it does give you a taste of the old miners' way of life.

But we have got to keep moving. We pass a Sammy Davis Jr home and eventually stop at the Hoover Dam. It is definitely vast. You are told of the people who gave their lives in building such a structure. There is even a plaque dedicated to a dog. But the reason I am speeding up my tales is to tell you of our next stop. I have always wanted to come here and have been excited about the place whenever I have seen it on films or heard the name mentioned.

You see, you just come out of the dust and into an oasis of lights, colours, spectaculars, glamour and sheer imagination and of dreams coming true. This is none other than Las Vegas. 'Viva

Las Vegas', as Elvis sang, and he was just one of the many guests and celebrities to appear here over the years. It is a wonderful place and somewhere that you can get completely lost in. Where daytime can become night. This is neon light city in the desert.

You can pull one-arm bandits for as long as you like. All around are people hitting jackpots. One casino boasted a jackpot every minute, and they do. But hundreds are playing. I won a little on every machine I played but if you keep playing the money can soon go back. The noise is also quite incredible, the chinking sound of coins hitting the collecting bin, the levers being pulled, the drums rolling, the sirens sounding on a big win, people telling of their win or their bad luck, shouts and laughter. This place has all the human emotions and, of course, lights of all colours flashing; stars light up. I cannot think of the electricity bill for this area. It must be colossal!

One big old slot machine must have been 12ft high by 6ft wide. A dollar a go. I just had to have one pull; nothing. In one place a glass case just sits there, no security, inside for everybody to see. US$ 1,000,000. They work on the theory that if you steal it they will catch you in the desert, as there is nowhere else to go. Once there was a whole row of machines with nobody playing them – about 30 machines in all. I had a pack of 25 cents and ran along putting one coin in each machine, pulling the arm and moving onto the next one. It was exhilarating racing along, putting the coin in, pulling the moving as fast as possible. I won nothing until the last machine, then hit a jackpot of about US$5. Basically, I had broken even. You can also play craps, throwing a pair of dice or Black Jack (Pontoon) or chance your

WHAT A WAY TO TRAVEL

luck on the roulette table. In some of the casinos we were given free drinks. They will do anything to keep you in their place and spending money. But actually you can get just as much enjoyment watching others spending their money, sharing their losses and celebrating with them when they win. There is so much going on, so much to do and so much to see, and you may even get lucky!

Las Vegas is definitely a fun place with so much entertainment. You can take in all sorts of shows from famous singers and acts to circus shows out on the streets. We came across the original Al Capone's Cadillac with its reinforced metal plating and bullet-proof windows. It was magic to touch it and to think back to the days of Chicago and gangsters; and then there is Caesar's Palace. The place is unbelievable. It is incredible. As you approach by night it has a long driveway with beautiful fountains lit by white lights. Along the sidewalks are fir trees and the palace is lit by a light green light. Outside are statues and you enter by escalator which passes holograms of a princess welcoming you to Caesar's Palace. Inside are tables, machines and waitresses dressed in white togas and crowns, serving you on silver trays. Oh boy, there is certainly money in this place. You can just tell by the way people dress. I love the names of these places: Silver City, Star Dust, Frontier, Continental, Silver Slipper, Circus, Tropicana, Aladdin, Flamingo, Sands, Desert Inn, Riviera, Dunes and many, many more.

Now there is an uptown and downtown to Vegas, connected by the Strip. Along the Strip there are many Chapels of Love, places where you can get married, quickly and cheaply but I

WHAT A WAY TO TRAVEL

think quite romantic. When you reach downtown there is the Horseshoe, Pioneer Club, Mint, Coin Castle and the famous wooden carving of the cowboy who waves and the cowgirl with her hat and her legs crossed, and when they light up they look great. Chanced my arm one more time on the roulette table and won over US$200. I could not resist purchasing a little china loo. On the lid it said, 'I crapped out in Las Vegas'. Brilliant visit but now it is time to move on.

We are heading from where the legends come from, cowboy country, names like Jesse and Frank James, Wyatt Earp, Doc Holliday, Billy the Kid and many others. We stopped at an old Gold Rush town known now as a Ghost Town. It was just like the movies, tumbleweed in the streets, wooden bars to tie your horse to, and an old saloon where the doors flapped open independently either side. You could imagine that gunfights took place in this very street. As we arrived one of our fellow travellers was arrested by the local sheriff with handcuffs but released very quickly.

We headed for the saloon. Above on the walls were drawings of the famous cowboys, some outlaws, and even a sheriff who had been down this way before. The whole place had a unique atmosphere. I purchased some fool's gold contained in a little sack pouch with the words 'Nuggets from California' printed on it.

Leaving the town we enter Death Valley, a sun-kissed desert road where in the summer the temperature can soar up to 130°C. The road dipped up and down for 8 miles. This is where they test rocket engines and the space shuttle lands. It is so empty for miles. Today we cannot go through the pass because it snowed last night. Only 85 miles away they had snow while we have 90° heat.

Eventually made it to Yosemite National Park. Huge trees you can drive through the trunk, waterfalls, this is bear country and the views are magnificent. It is so lush and green. Ideal for camping out or picnicking. Came down Snake Pass with over 200 bends and extremely steep. Passing Columbia and the old 49ers gold miners and gold mines, plus the town of Jackson, lumber cutting county. Going on up to 7,000ft with snow still on the mountaintops; stayed the night around Lake Tahoe.

An early start took us through Sacramento, the state capital of California. We travelled over the Oakland Bay Bridge and arrived in San Francisco early afternoon.

The city tour included the Golden Gate Bridge, which was celebrating its 50th birthday today. On the news later it said over 200,000 people walked over it today, causing massive traffic jams. In the evening fireworks would be let off to celebrate. What good fortune to arrive today. We drove around Fisherman's Wharf but would come back on foot. We were taken to a hillside where we had a view of the whole city and also caught a glimpse of the Pacific Ocean for the first time.

Upon our return to the hotel we decided to explore the city by foot. It can be tough going. Do you remember the film *Bullitt*, starring Steve McQueen, and the car chase up and down those hills? Well, that is how steep the hills are. We went to No. 1 Nob Hill, taking into account the hill and my body was only about 30 degrees apart. It was tough going. On top of the hill is

WHAT A WAY TO TRAVEL

a fantastic hotel with incredible decor. The Luxury Room cost US$750 per night. Luckily, it had been booked! We decided to take the cable cars down as they are fun to jump on and off The evening we spent in Chinatown where we enjoyed a delicious meal. It was massive and wonderful. Early to bed as we have a long day tomorrow.

Today we were going to Alcatraz, an island that was a high security prison. As you go off the boat it is quite eerie. Think of the murderers, kidnappers, criminals and gangsters that have walked this way before.

I found this an incredible and fascinating trip. We saw Al Capone's cell, the Bird Man of Alcatraz. We were told the famous escape which was shown on film by Clint Eastwood – *Escape from Alcatraz*. The model heads that were used are still displayed in their beds. We went through the shower area and into the exercise yard. But the most scary of all was being put into an isolation cell and having the door closed behind you. It is totally pitch black. I tried to walk from one end to the other and it is terrifying. I was just so glad to be released and the sunlight blinds you. Imagine being locked up in there for a long period of time. Touching the cell bars and seeing how small the cells are, it really must have been a horrendous place to be in.

Freezing cold water with a strong undercurrent surrounds the island. They say that if you escape off of the island the water would actually get you. There is one story of a prisoner who escaped on the laundry boat. Unfortunately for him the route was changed that day and instead of escaping it actually brought him back to Alcatraz.

WHAT A WAY TO TRAVEL

That certainly was a memorable trip and well recommended, but it was now time for lunch and there is no better place for a fish dinner than Fisherman's Wharf, Pier 39. It is a hive of activity, really packed out, certainly a popular place to eat. There are rides for the children and souvenir shops to peruse. I purchased a little white mug with a picture of a prisoner on it behind bars stating, 'I spent time on Alcatraz'. Also a black and white T-shirt with the name Alcatraz (there is a story later about this very T-shirt). I also found my name tag, 'BRANDON CALIFORNIA' and matches 'MADE IN SAN FRANCISCO FOR BRAD'. Oh, and a lighter, 'Property of Alcatraz Penitentiary'. Later I bought a white sweater with a San Francisco badge on it.

Just by the pier is an old Second World War submarine, which you can board and go below. A commentary is given for each room you enter. Conditions must have been very cramped for the men and it must have been a strange feeling being so deep in the ocean with so much water above you and no daylight. Watching a film tonight, *Beverly Hills Cop II*.

We have had some of our photographs developed. There is a brilliant assortment but there are two that stick out to me. One was hanging through the cell bars with my hands and arms. It really does look as though I am in prison. The second actually sitting on a hard mattress in a cell with a small wash basin and tiny toilet and the holes above which the men who escaped had crawled through.

We are on the move again. Today we are taking a drive along the coastline. This is the most scenic route in the world and the one place above all others, if I had a choice of where to live then this would be it!

WHAT A WAY TO TRAVEL

Starting at Pebble Beach and the 17-mile drive. A fantastic climate, fresh air, the sea rolling in onto beaches or jagged rocks. There are cliffs, alcoves and bays, Cyprus trees, golf courses, golden sands, seals in the sea, birds in the sky and squirrels running everywhere. It is so peaceful and very picturesque. No wonder Clint Eastwood lives here. We saw his home facing out to the ocean. We drove down and into Carmel at the time when Clint Eastwood was Mayor of this beautiful town. We even visited his restaurant and on the menu was a 12-ounce Magnum Force steak, and for just a few dollars extra a 16-ounce steak. Very clever, as they were named after two of his films. Unfortunately he was not about that day.

Kept following the coast road towards Los Angeles where the trip had begun. Passing Santa Barbara, stopping at Malibu Beach just to touch the golden sand and watch the sea rolling in, passed Joan Collins' home and the Hearst Castle. Also along the way was President Reagan's ranch.

Reached LA with a couple of days left before returning home. So we decided to take a coach down to Mexico.

Stopping at San Diego on the way down, we also saw the ship the Queen Mary dock.

Crossing the border found us all having to go through customs and passports but as we entered bright colours hit us. The Mexicans were wearing brightly coloured sombreros. We travelled to a town called Tijuana. There was a great deal of poverty and begging in the streets, an extremely poor area. But the people were friendly and would sell you anything. There is so much shopping to be done and the prices are very

WHAT A WAY TO TRAVEL

much reduced compared to the USA I purchased a Mexican man doll dressed in black with his poncho over his shoulder and sombrero tipped back, with 'Mexico' written inside. Also, a large sombrero with the Mexican flag dangling downwards, together with a souvenir photograph wearing a sombrero with 'Mexico' written on it, sitting on a colourful trailer with an ass pulling it and above it said, 'Tijuana 1987 Mexico'. The visit was a strange and different type of place with lots of colour and activity. But it is dirty and there is so much poverty you really cannot ignore, although it is still an experience I enjoyed and well worth a visit. It also gives you a flavour of the Mexican way of life.

Our last day. We went to the top of the hotel – the sunroof where we sunbathed and swam in the pool. We had a great view of LA and Ringo Starr had a home just behind us, which was situated in the hills. As we lay sunbathing we reflected back on our trip. It had been a fantastic three weeks. We had seen so much and accomplished loads, although it was all completed at high speed. But worth every penny, which we paid, and we went over the list.

Los Angeles, Sunset Strip, Beverly Hills, Hollywood, Chinese Theatre, Universal Studios, Disneyland, a desert, the Grand Canyon, Las Vegas, cowboy and Indian country, ghost towns, goldmines, forests, national park, bear country, San Francisco, Alcatraz, Monterey, Carmel and Mexico. We had seen so many famous houses; we had visited California in true style, Nevada, Arizona, and taken home loads of souvenirs, photographs and, most of all, our memories.

CRUISING THE CARIBBEAN

I have always been a sun lover. You could say I even worship the sun. Being a Leo star sign I have no problem lounging in the sun all day, and there is no better way of tanning than cruising. On board ship you lay on the sun decks and top up the tan between ports, you are fed well, and when you hit different ports you can lay out on some of the best beaches in the world boasting the clearest sea you will ever find. Plus every island has its own unique atmosphere and way of life. Joining the ship in Miami the party time started. Everybody is out for a good time, which leads to a party atmosphere on board ship, and it is very easy to make new friends. I was to share a cabin but the guy I am to share with is an employee of the company and will not be joining until the Cayman Islands.

Our itinerary: first port of call Labadee, Haiti; San Juan, Puerto Rico; St Thomas, United States Virgin Islands; Ocho Rios, Jamaica; George Town, Grand Cayman; Cozumel, Mexico and back to Miami, Florida.

What can I say about Labadee? It is just so beautiful with its white sands, swaying palm trees, the sea so clear with its changes in colour depending on the depth, and it is warm. It is honestly like taking a warm bath. There is no big toe dipping over here; it really is straight in. Labadee is paradise for those

WHAT A WAY TO TRAVEL

who are fond of the active life. Among the activities available are aquabikes, paddle boats, swimming and snorkelling.

Along the beach are the local traders who sell huge seashells. Then I found a hammock. I had always dreamed of me swinging in a hammock in between two trees on a Caribbean island with white sands, scorching hot, just gently swaying to and fro. Mind you, getting into it was not as easy as I had thought and getting out was not too good, either. But there it is, I have done it. Two photographs were taken, one completely lying down with one arm in the air, the other with one foot on the ground. Sometimes on cold winter nights at home I look at those photographs and it sort of warms me up inside. A dream of paradise island and I am on it, loving every minute.

I found in a book a photograph of the Sun Viking, our ship anchored in the turquoise waters of Columbus Cove at Labadee, which is the Royal Caribbean's Private Paradise. You can see the green mountainside, the different blues of the sea and the white sand. It is just incredible, and I left my footprints there.

PUERTO RICO - SAN JUAN

Columbus landed on this island in November 1493. Puerto Rico stands for Rich Port. There is a very strong Spanish influence. Spanish is the official language but almost everybody speaks English too. The currency is US$. There is an incredible old castle built between 1539–1783. The streets are compact and people shop for bargains. I found some magnificent metal magnetic fish, incredible colours and brightly coloured, stamped with Puerto Rico.

WHAT A WAY TO TRAVEL

Our next port of call the US Virgin Islands, St. Thomas. Now remember, this was pirate country, famous names like Bluebeard, Blackbeard and Drake sailed around these waters, but I was more interested in what was under the water. I had booked up a submarine dive. We took the local ferry out to meet the submarine 'Atlantis 3', which held about 100 people, and you dive to a depth of about 80ft. It is an especially reinforced submarine. There is no need for oxygen or preparing to dive. It is just get in, lock the hatch and dive, dive, dive. It is an incredible feeling, going deeper and deeper. The views are wonderful. On the outside divers are feeding the fish so all shapes and sizes of fish surround the submarine and the colours of the fish are unbelievable. There are shades of colour I have never seen before, bright yellows that are transparent, pinks and blues and greens. I cannot describe it and, what with the movement, it is totally fascinating to watch. As you go deeper you see the coral with its life and colour. There are also bigger fish about. Turtles were sinking slowly to eat the grass at the bottom of the seabed. We were taken around an old shipwreck lying on the bottom with little fish swimming in and out of crevices. A 4ft long fish passed right by my window with his big old eyes jerking around and his mouth opening and closing. It is fantastic down here, certainly another world! Suddenly from the left-hand side a shark appeared, scanning the area. It swam right under the submarine, out the other side and just disappeared into the darkness. This is an incredible experience and they gave us a certificate to prove our dive into the sparkling waters of the Caribbean.

WHAT A WAY TO TRAVEL

Back on shore I found incredible postcards which captured the coral and the fish with their unique colours.

In the afternoon back on board ship, an amazing thing happened. The sun was completely blocked out; this is called a corona. It happens when moisture gathers towards the sun and completely covers it. This was another first for me.

At the dinner table while my fellow passengers talked about their day and the corona I, however, went on and on about the submarine, the fish, the turtles, the shark and the magnificent colours. Unfortunately dinner was turtle or shark fin soup followed with fish. How could I eat my new-found little friends? No, only joking, the meal was steak – thank goodness!

Actually got quite burnt today, glowing in the dark like a lobster, so I suppose you can say I had quite a fishy day today?

OCHO RIOS - JAMAICA

Jamaica – no, she went by herself! An old joke, but this place is no joke. Home of reggae, Bob Marley, Rastafarians and the love of cricket.

First, we joined a coach tour. The island does have pockets of poverty and filthiness but it is rich in plantations and the warmth of the people. We were taken into a garden area situated high on a hilltop. The flowers were so beautiful, watching a hummingbird drink from a flower; the place seems to have a mixture of exquisite scenery mixed with shanty-type shacks.

We headed for Dunn's River Falls. You walk down these broken steps. On reaching the bottom as you look up it is fantastic watching the cascading water. The top seems some

100 yards away. The guide advised us to jump in, hold hands, as we were about to climb the Falls. And we did. Some parts were dangerous and slippery, others were very deep and you could not see what you were standing on. Some places you stood under the waterfall and let the water just fall all over you. It is fantastic fun and a real buzz when you reach the top.

Now the saying here is, 'No problem'. You can buy the T-shirt with it on. The locals can speak the dialect that you just cannot understand. They are ever so friendly but can be scary at times. Back to the ship we sang some lovely local songs we were taught as we started to peel and blister. It is hot, man!

GRAND CAYMAN ISLAND

I met a lady from here once who bet me I would never visit Grand Cayman because it is so far from anywhere. Well, she would have lost her bet.

It is beautiful, like a quaint old-fashioned fishing village but it is so clean and the people really friendly. It has a seven-mile stretch of sandy beaches and the souvenir shopping is brilliant. It is mostly from the sea; shells made into rings, replica turtles and sharks. There is even a place called 'Hell'. It is hot here. After ten steps I am sweating up.

Back on board ship it is party night. Talent contest. Our whole table decides to dress up as each other. The names were put into a hat. I pulled out Peggy so that night I put her dress on, jewellery, and make-up, painted my nails and applied my lipstick and went to dinner. We all just laughed and laughed at each other dressed as somebody else. We came nowhere in the contest so I went back to the cabin to change. My new roommate had let himself in. Can you imagine the look on his face as I entered the room dressed like a transvestite? Believe me, it took a bit of explaining but Rick was great. He was a top accountant for the Royal Caribbean Shipping Line and became a great travelling companion. We shared many a late night with a beer, and our mutual love of chess gave us some great games and competition.

MEXICO - COZUMEL

We visited just after a hurricane had blown a path across this stretch of land so there was quite a bit of rebuilding in force.

But today was a perfect day with no clouds, the sky blue and the weather was hot and sunny. I tried walking around a bit to get the flavour of the place but it was so hot so I decided to hit the beach. I enquired about scuba diving but was told you do not need to here, just stick your head in the water and you will see as many fish as you desire. Surely they're kidding? but they are not. I only walked out about 10 yards. I had brought with me my swimming goggles and stuck my head in. I could not believe the sight that met my eyes. The fish were all around me, in between my legs, over my feet and coming right up to my goggles. It was incredible. You could see so much and they were not afraid of you, but try as I may to touch them, there is no way as they are always one step ahead of you. I tried and tried but they just accelerate a little and you just miss. I was in the water looking at them for hours.

Well, this was our last port of call. It has been a fascinating journey. I have enjoyed each and every port of call and compared the difference in the way of life, styles and savoured the scenery. Also the people and glorious weather, but what really made it so special is the ship. Cruising the Caribbean is fabulous, the entertainment, food and service is first class. I have just had so much fun and although I travelled alone I was never alone!

My table friends were brilliant and it was extremely pleasing to have met them. At the end of the voyage a woman from the next table approached our table and congratulated us for having such a happy and friendly table. She confessed that each day she would listen to our conversations, as her own table was so dull and boring. That made us all feel fantastic.

Peggy, Mary, Diana and Rick (my roommate) were all about to meet again, on shore and by a stroke of luck!

Now, do you remember Kelly, the young 16-year-old I had met at Disneyworld? Well, we had become very good penfriends over the last six years. When I disembark the ship Kelly will be waiting for me and, oh boy, was I in for a surprise? This young 16-year-old was now a beautiful, slim 22-year-old and gorgeous, too. And what with my 10-day tan I looked ok as well.

We just hit it off as soon as we met. We went to a nearby hotel garden and spent all afternoon drinking and talking. Now Peggy, Mary and Diana had a hotel booked for a full day and night but would only be using it for half a day. So we looked it up and knocked on the door. We had a great couple of hours talking about our trip and meeting Kelly. That evening we phoned Rick and his wife. They took us out around Miami.

ORLANDO - FLORIDA

Kelly had hired a convertible car and it was great fun, with the wind blowing your hair travelling at speed towards Orlando, which was to be my home for the next month. Kelly's friend Bill gave us free roam of his house and a bedroom. Outhouse snakes and an occasional alligator had known to be out the back. There was a BBQ, a large lawn and a lake, where swimming was not recommended. This was one hell of a party group and I mean, could they party. They also enjoyed their drink; this next month was to be one of the best months of my life. I just had so much fun and laughter. The group was a fantastic bunch and they accepted me into their lives. We went to discos, nightclubs, pool halls, bars, swimming pool parties, dinghy days, beach days and once while on a visit to the beach we watched the space shuttle take off The ground literally vibrated and we were miles away. The acceleration was so great it disappeared very quickly.

We even had oyster bar nights and bars with local singers who changed words to popular songs and made them catching and funny. Sometimes at 3 or 4 in the morning we would go to Denny's to eat or tacos at a Mexican restaurant. Quite often we were at happy hour that lasted all night.

During the month people came and went all of the time. I met so many funny and interesting people. Then I met friends of friends. I had a super time. The girls and guys certainly worked hard and played hard. I really got an insight into the American way of life and I had lived it gaining enough memories to last a lifetime.

However, my holiday was not over yet. After tearful farewells I had to catch the Greyhound bus back down to Miami, but I will be back.

WHAT A WAY TO TRAVEL

You see, my brother Steve had just completed a trip from New York to San Francisco and he was flying into Miami. We had ordered a mobile home camper and planned on touring the Florida Keys.

We missed each other at the airport but met up at a hotel where the camper was parked. We sat and talked about our recent experiences for hours. Then we re-checked our plans and headed for the Keys.

First stop Key Largo; it was the first time Steve had observed the fish under the sea. He loved it as much as I did. There was an old sunken galleon with original cannons on board. We had great fun going from one Key area to another. There are over 21 different little Key areas, some are for fishing, others have aquariums or dolphin shows, and some are boat builders or sell from small shops. At one of the stops, the John Pennekamp Coral Reef State Park, below the water is a statue of Christ with his arms outstretched and lifting up. A barracuda swam between Steve's legs.

We crossed the longest bridge in the world (7 miles) and eventually arrived at Key West, which is the furthest point. We made our way back up the Keys and headed for Fort Lauderdale, which is the beginning of 47 miles of continuous beaches.

First, we pulled onto Miami Beach, fantastic beaches and swimming. We kept going on the beach road through Palm Beach and up to the John F Kennedy Space Centre. Finally I introduced brother Steve to the friends I had made in Orlando before we returned the camper and took our flight home. But I am certainly coming back.

SINGAPORE, JAVA AND BALI

SINGAPORE

Due to hard work and a little stroke of good luck I have just won a trip for two. At work, together with 50 other couples. First stop: Singapore. It is quite a long flight but you will be going to the Far East, taking in Malaysia and Indonesia.

In Singapore our hotel is the Dynasty, a smashing hotel. From the outside it is like a hexagonal tower going skywards and is a great landmark. The reception area is the highest I have ever seen. The walls are well decorated. The hotel is certainly first class.

The first evening everybody was shepherd downtown. We did not know why until we actually got there. But what a sight awaited us. There must have been over a hundred men sitting on bikes with a type of combination bucket seat attached to the bike. They were to give us a circular tour around the block. Our group, of course, saw this as an opportunity for a race. Everybody went scrambling for one of the younger men. I jumped in on an old boy but we got a flying start. It was brilliant. People overtaking on the inside, outside, two wheels up around the corners, photographing each other, cutting in front or braking hard. We pretended to whip our drivers to get more speed and I must say the bike riders really entered into the spirit of it all. I did not win but was well up at the front. It was great fun and the winner got the biggest tip.

Our next stop was the famous Raffles Hotel. We were shown onto the Garden Lawn and served the famous original Singapore Sling drink. Quite delicious. My uncle stood outside the Raffles Hotel during the Second World War. It is a privilege to be standing in his footsteps.

JAVA

Known as a third world country, there is a high percentage of poverty but you could never tell by the hospitality of the people. Our hotel was said to be one of the best on the island and it was super, trying the differences in food. Kebabs with all types of dips. The humidity is incredible. While we were in town a motor scooter passed me with the wife and husband on and five children. It is fascinating watching their lifestyles, their music and culture. We were taken to an ancient palace by horse-drawn carriage. When you enter through the Royal Archway you are met by a crescendo of music, little old men dressed in white sit crumpled on the floor with their legs crossed. I got the feeling they had all been smoking something, as they seemed to string anything that was in front of them whenever they liked. There seemed to be no written music to follow, put all together, it is a fascinating mixture of noise. It is actually absorbing and very catchy.

The Far East is so different from our way of life. It is fascinating watching and observing the differences. That evening we were taken to a local exhibition of dance and music.

WHAT A WAY TO TRAVEL

The colour, which is portrayed, is spectacular, bright yellows and reds. And the way they move is unique. They have style and grace and perform ancient old dances that have been passed down from generation to generation.

BALI

This is like a paradise island, but what do people mean by paradise? Well, the weather is a must. Bali has an incredible climate. It is hot and humid. The beach area is fine white sand; beautiful warm waters, although they can be dangerous with sea urchins and snakes. The plantation around, palm trees, greenery, first-class hotels with excellent food and service. Well, Bali has this and more. It has one bonus: the people with their politeness, honesty, smiles and the welcoming atmosphere is special plus the entertainment. You will see dancing and hear music that you will not see and hear anywhere else in the world.

You know when you have arrived somewhere completely different the moment that you arrive. At the hotel music and the most beautiful girls in the world welcome you. Beauty in their honesty and complicity, their brightly coloured long sarongs. You are greeted with a necklace of flowers placed over your head. And as you sip on your long cool drink you are mesmerised by their dancing to a strong beat of a drum, to the chinking of instruments, to the pipes. The women sort of dipped in their stance move, the hips are greatly swayed, the arms snake around, the fingers pointing and the hands fanning skywards gently twist and move around. The head does little jerking movements or goes slowly to one side whereas the eyes

WHAT A WAY TO TRAVEL

are looking starwards. It is an amazing combination and so fascinating to watch. The hotel itself is truly reminiscent of a Balinese temple. During our stay we saw Balinese history and folklore reenacted for us in the form of music and dance, and excursions to craft centres including the wood carvers of Mas and the silversmiths of Celuk. We also saw the monkey dance ceremony: many men dancing, some dressed with monkey masks.

When you hit the local markets there are so many bargains to be found. The clothes, for example, are so well made, colourful with such a multiple of choice. I purchased six pairs of cotton trousers, blues, pinks, yellows and black and they have still survived to this day, including different coloured tops to match.

On one of the field trips to a temple, Julie and I went for a walk off of the beaten track. We ended up in the outback. We saw the little bamboo shacks which the locals called home, with no electricity or running water. Women with their children bathing in a stream and washing their clothes. Unfortunately we got very lost and in those temperatures were very glad to make it back to the group.

The Balinese will sell anything they have got at any time, in the restaurant, on a balcony; they would throw their wares up to you. You would either throw it back or some money instead. At one time, sitting down for a meal, a blue top came whizzing over and landed in a bowl of soup. Once on a beach ladies carrying baskets and wearing straw hats approached a group of us. They asked if you would like a massage. The whole group agreed they would. Our ladies took their tops or dresses off, just in their

WHAT A WAY TO TRAVEL

knickers and bras; some did not have bras. The ladies began the massages with different creams and oils for certain parts of the body. The odours given off smelt fantastic, coconuts wafted through the air. Then it was the turn of the men. My lady had the number 69 on her hat. She rubbed me, stroked me, squeezed my muscles, and turned me over. It was ever so relaxing and yet invigorating until she bent my legs back up to my head to finish me off. The cost was about one English pound each. Great fun and good photographs taken.

On one of the many evenings' entertainment the whole group was asked to dress as one of the locals. We were supplied with our sarongs wrapped around our waists and no shoes on. Everybody got out new tops we had purchased at the market plus our straw hats that looked like pyramids on our heads. But our winning stroke of genius was the make-up. We painted on our long dangling moustaches, red blusher and slightly slanted our eyes. Holding our hands together as though in prayer and grinning, showing our teeth and gently bowing, we all looked the part.

It was a superb evening. Everybody dressed up, a superb meal served and great music and dance, but unknown to me all managers were to be thrown into the swimming pool. Being a manager myself I was in for an early bath. Even my mascara ran that night!

What else can I say about the island of Bali? OK, maybe the flight's a little long but it is like a rainbow. At the end of the rainbow is a pot of gold. Bali, all those miles to see those incredible smiles.

WHAT A WAY TO TRAVEL

I have got some amazing photographs of our group, sitting and standing in around the pool area, sipping on drinks, coconuts floating in the water with straws protruding out, sunglasses and bikinis and swimsuits. Everybody looks so happy and relaxed. A good time was certainly had by all.

BRAZIL - SOUTH AMERICA

Our group enjoyed the trip so much to Bali that for the next year we worked extremely hard with long hours, but it was all worthwhile. Our reward was a free trip for two to Latin America, first stop Rio de Janeiro, Brazil.

We arrived late evening in Rio de Janeiro. On our coach trip to the hotel one of the first sights we saw was Christ the Redeemer high on a hilltop overlooking the city. The statue was well lit. It almost beams out to you like a halo as if the light comes from the heavens above. With His outstretched arms and palms facing upwards it is as though He is welcoming you to the city and you have His blessing.

Our hotel is huge with magnificent gardens and a large swimming pool area with a bar in the centre. Looks like I am going to run up a large bar bill.

The first two days we all just relaxed around the pool, soaking up the rays and getting over the time difference and jet lag. We did piggy back races, diving competitions and on one occasion I wore my white thong. An American lady approached me and asked if I would pose for her to picture me in my tiny bathing suit. I was in my element, posing while she snapped away. She reckoned I had a great butt.

After two days we began to wonder if this was the Rio

WHAT A WAY TO TRAVEL

everybody talked about. I mean, you could do what we were doing anywhere. I need not have worried, as the holiday was about to take off in a big way.

It started with a trip to Sugar Loaf mountain. The rock is so steep yet so narrow. It is like a thumb on your hand sticking upwards with nothing around it. A cable car takes you right to the top. I felt a little jellified as looking down you really do not realise just how high this is. But when you get to the top the view is so worthwhile you can span all of Rio, the high rise, and the bays, the beaches and harbour. A photograph on top was taken of Julia and I and etched into a plate dish with Rio above. A great souvenir. Once we hit ground and found our feet we were off to the famous Copacabana Beach, a wide and long stretch of golden sand, and everything happens here. Volleyball, weightlifting, posing, bird watching and the smallest bikinis in the world. From the back they just seem to disappear between the cheeks and, because it is a multi-racial society, you can see every shade of colour from chalk white to red to tan to bronze to jet black. Why is Copacabana Beach so famous? Well, it is not just the beach it is what is on it that counts, and everybody runs alongside it!

We were taken to the local markets, so colourful and interesting with local arts, crafts and paintings. I purchased some great tops and diamonds. So many couples in the group got engaged or bought eternity rings.

That evening we took in a local show. It was like no other I have ever been to. There were the topless dancers, the dresses worn were like those from carnivals, the colour and sparkle, the

WHAT A WAY TO TRAVEL

long flowing gowns, the feathers and jewellery, the crowns, the head gear and hats made an incredible spectacle. Then came the transvestites dressed as women in much the same clothes. Well, I for one found it hard to tell the difference. There was singing, dancing and parades but above all the music moved you. The Samba, Rumba, Tango, the maracas, the tambourine, drums and cymbals. You could not help but tap a foot or want to get up and let yourself go. This whole evening gave me such a lift; now I really knew I was in Rio, Brazil.

The next day we were off to a football match. Two local rival teams were to play each other. The stadium was larger than Wembley and the crowds are fantastic. It was a two-tier stadium and there were flags and banners everywhere. The singing and drums can be deafening. Due to the fact the supporters are so packed in, it is impossible to move. To say you want to spend a penny, well it is custom to fill a cup if you are on, say, the top balcony, and throw it over onto the cheaper seats below. Luckily we were sheltered. When the teams took to the pitch the fans went wild with excitement and when a goal was scored they went crazy, but their football was so exciting to watch. Mind you, when I came out I was deaf from all those whistles being blown. The score was 2-2.

That evening we spent in an outdoor restaurant by Copacabana Beach. It is so warm and the lights of Rio make it such a romantic city, and souvenir sellers can harass you.

Today we were off to a deserted island for a beach BBQ. Unfortunately the weather took a change for the worse. The heavens opened up. We all got completely drenched. All day it poured with rain, and when it pours here it really does pour. On our return to the centre the roads were flooded. Parts of the hillside had been washed away. There were power cuts everywhere; traffic was at a standstill. The road had opened up and swallowed cars. The whole place was awash!

Well, today we are leaving Rio temporarily and going further inland by flight to Manaus. We are going deep into Amazonas, jungle country, and to find and trace the source of the Amazon.

The hotel is superb. It has its own built-in zoo, local animals from the surrounding area, monkeys, parrots and cats. Although I am not a zoo fanatic it does give you a chance to observe from close quarters and to see their bright colours and mannerisms.

There is a beautiful swimming pool with palm trees and the whole surrounding area and gardens are tropical. There is so much rain and sunlight and moist atmosphere. Everything grows so well and in too huge proportions. Around the pool is the local pet parrot. I had my arm outstretched when he was put onto my hand. God, he is so heavy I could barely stand the weight. I had to support my arm and he loved to give a playful nip. There were a couple of birds in the tree. Well, you know what they say: 'A bird in your hand is worth two in the bush.'

Now the serious stuff. We were taken deep into the jungle where we met tribal Indians and observed their way of life. Straw huts with outside cooking pots. I do not know who observed most, them or us. This bamboo type hut housed the arts, crafts and souvenirs of the local people. We purchased bows and arrows, big seed containers decorated with feathers and handles, which when shaken give off a sound like the sea

WHAT A WAY TO TRAVEL

waves breaking onto stones. Also a home-made necklace of different kinds of seed pods. Placed in the middle a full set of piranha teeth, so large and sharp. Also there was a stuffed and pickled piranha. A group of us with our souvenirs and no tops on danced and wailed in simulated Indian voices. Dancing on the spot, spinning around and lifting one leg, we really did look and sound like the local tribes. But I am not sure the locals would agree, but it must have been pretty good as a rain dance because later on that day it was to rain for two days solid.

We visited a local floating restaurant only for tourists and took a dip in a supposedly safe pool. Mind you, we did have piranhas on our minds, but it was hot so in we went. One guy with telescopic lenses on his camera noticed a floating log. On further investigation it was proved to be a crocodile no more than 50 yards from the swimmers. The alarm was given and I have never seen people move so fast. The men got out first and hauled the women out. The crocodile took no notice and swam slowly away. Nobody went back into the water.

We were taken along a narrow winding path to see an animal sanctuary. The setting was fantastic. All around was deep, thick rain forest that actually speaks to you through the cries and shrieks of the animals and birds. And occasionally one would fly out and all the cameras clicked. The sanctuary held leopards, pumas and tigers. You could actually touch one through the netting or if it yawned you saw its massive teeth. One fascination we found was a group of ants. They were huge in size, going about their chores, carrying leaves ten times their own size.

We were taken on the water on small boats and advised it

was probably best not to put our hands into the water. You can imagine that filled me with confidence but it was a picturesque setting until the rain started. Then it poured down. Just goes to show that rain dance worked.

Our next leg of the journey was a local ferry ride for quite a few miles down the Amazon to where the rivers meet. It is unique and incredible. The two rivers do not join until miles later. This is shown in the colours. Due to temperature differences of the two rivers, one being darker than the other, and sludge and silt that one picks up. The two colours run parallel to each other, the colours do not mix. It is fast running and looks like two different colours and two different rivers that never meet. However, they eventually break each other down and mix into one.

We saw the biggest lily pads in the world. Some are more than 10ft wide. You feel as though you could walk on them.

Back to the hotel. I was so glad we made this part of the trip. It gave you another slant on Brazil and a totally different way of life.

When you awake early in the morning and go outside, the trees are covered in a light mist. The sun is rising and breaking through, clearing the mist, and the animals are waking and calling to each other.

We were back off to Rio to finish off our tans and enjoy the last few days in Brazil. From this vacation I have got superb photographs of all my work colleagues, wives, girlfriends, all lounging around pools while it is winter back at home. There is me in my thong, beaches, animals, jungles, rivers, dance shows. To me, Brazil is colourful, musical and it has a rhythm.

WHAT A WAY TO TRAVEL

One of the bonuses of these long-haul flights is that you get to go to some offbeat countries, which normally you would not get to see. Quite often you are allowed off the plane to shop and look around, although confined to the airport. It is like saying, 'Well at least you have been to places like the United Arab Emirates, Oman and Dubai.'

FROM HARLOW TO HONG KONG

THE NETHERLANDS, WEST AND EAST GERMANY, POLAND, RUSSIA INNER AND OUTER MONGOLIA, CHINA, HONG KONG

This to me and my brother Steve is the most amazing trip we have ever taken. It has everything and more. Let me explain.

Standing at Harlow Town station early one morning with our cases packed, we took our first photograph. About to board the train to Liverpool Station. It was to be the first train of many as our final destination was to be Hong Kong and it is trains all of the way.

At the hotel in London, over breakfast we met our fellow travellers on the extravaganza. They came from all walks of life and countries. There were Americans, New Zealanders, Australians, Cayman Islands, French, Scottish, and Welsh. There were couples, single travellers and solo lady travellers. About 40 in total. Plus Hans from Holland who was to be a guide all of the way.

A train took us to Harwich where we crossed by ferry to the Hook of Holland and started our journey heading across Europe.

The train compartment becomes our home, restaurant, bed and study. First pick-up was boxes of food at a station. We all helped to get them on board and shared out the contents which

WHAT A WAY TO TRAVEL

consisted of plastic knives, fork, spoons, biscuits, rolls, tea bags, sugar, packed lunches. Now we know why we had the big breakfast because on the train you will never be sure where your next meal will come from.

What a fantastic group this is. We have got some real characters. Two French ladies who speak no English and young and old mixing together. It is a fantastic blend of people. Everybody so caring and talkative, interesting too. The attitude is if you need anything, ask, and if they can help then they will.

The first couple of days we all got to know each other, swapping stories, telling each other of their backgrounds, why they were on the trip, stories, jokes and laughter. The train hardly made a noise as it went along. You certainly were not thrown around. At nighttime your beds were pulled down and made. Once in this, catch nets and straps were attached to catch you if you happened to be catapulted off your bunk.

There was constant hot water from a boiler heater so you could always get a cup of tea. If you wanted to stretch your legs you could always walk down the corridor, which was the length of the train. You would meet all types of travellers, Russians and Poles going home, people heading for meeting points, some had no compartment but open sleeping areas. The toilet area was a bit rough. Washing facilities are bare and you do not always manage to get hot water. But, what with the train's motion, it is difficult to shave and wash anyway. For 3 days I can live with that. Let's face it, everyone looks the same. All the men are sprouting beards, one guy called Stanley soaped up to shave, sat on the toilet then a guard let himself in and told Stanley to get out as we were pulling into a station and you are not allowed to use water in stations.

Another occasion I went into the loos, a little old Russian lady was on the toilet. I made my apologies and left; her face was a picture to see.

After passing through West Germany we approached the borders of East Berlin. At a very slow pace we trundled on. The Berlin Wall was very visible and there was an air of silence about, an intrigue; you could see the No-Man's Land between the barriers, the high turrets with guards perched high, barbed wire could be seen everywhere. There were the checkpoints and the grim reality of a country divided. We stopped at the Berlin Station. We had to risk the train pulling out without us as Steve and I were determined to stand on that station to be able to say we had stood *in* East Germany.

One of the big changes we observed from West to East was the housing conditions. They were more cramped and not so clean, but dull-looking. The cars parked outside the houses were completely different, all very much alike, older and smaller. You can sense a restricted way of life.

On this trip we were to get used to border guards, custom officials and soldiers coming into our compartments any time of day and night checking our paperwork, passports, luggage. I just did not realise they would check in the ceiling, under the seats, on the roof, under the carriage, between the wheels and you are not to smile as they take their job extremely seriously. I must say that I felt somewhat intimidated as they come across as very abrupt and aggressive, and if they said, 'Stand there!' you

WHAT A WAY TO TRAVEL

stood there without moving.

Well, the train kept moving; our cabin became the Swap Shop. Everybody came to us for everything and we took from him or her what they would not use; jams, butter, sugar etc. etc. Unfortunately our cabin became a bit of a tip and what with not showering or shaving we began to hum, but it all added to the fun of it all. However, when we visited the ladies cabins everything was tidy, clean and in its place. Put us to shame, but our excuse was that we were on holiday.

Crossed the Polish border, stopping at Warsaw. We had a wait of 20 minutes so most people got off The local children had gathered in droves and were asking for anything we did not want or need. We gave them everything we had; leftover food, sugar, sweets and biscuits, as we would be leaving the train soon for a few days.

At the station were some great old steam trains. They looked magnificent with their steam bellowing out. But the buzz was just to be in Poland and the capital to boot, Warsaw.

Our next landmark – the Russian border. After our customary border interrogation we were led to a side holding. You see that in Russia the gauge of the railway lines is different from that of most of Europe so the wheel sections on our train had to be changed. A lot of tapping and adjustments were being made then the whole train was lifted and the old wheels were pushed out and the new ones pushed into place. The train was lowered and locked back on. Peter the Welshman got on and said that we had just had our boogies changed. Steve at that time was just picking his nose so we found this quite funny.

WHAT A WAY TO TRAVEL

All of my life I had been interested in Russia, the Soviet Union, CCCP, and now I was within her borders. The landscape from the train was vast, hills and valleys, small towns and villages, tiny houses, on farmland wooded areas covered with golden yellow leaves, and we were on our way to the capital, Moscow, and probably the heart of communism and a super power of the world.

Our approach to Moscow station was mysterious and exciting in anticipation of our visit. We were taken by coach to our Intourist hotel with over 6,000 rooms –at one time the largest hotel in the world. We had little time to shower and unpack and to take our evening meal as we had been given tickets to watch the Bolshoi Ballet and it was important to be on time to get in. And here we were in Russia with all its sights to see, and we were off to see a ballet. I had never seen any ballet dancing and certainly would not have said I was a connoisseur or fan.

But the moment you enter the Bolshoi Theatre you know this is to be something special. This is the centre of ballet. The world's best only perform here to a very knowledgeable and appreciative audience. We were lucky to be early and took the opportunity to investigate the orchestra. It is fascinating watching their faces concentrating on their music sheets and finely tuning their instruments. We take our seats, the orchestra strikes up, the curtains open and then the movements and artistry of the dancers spellbind you. Not only are the dancers mesmerising but also the music and audience appreciation. It was a fantastic night of entertainment, highly recommended after all. The Bolshoi Ballet Company must be the most famous in the world.

WHAT A WAY TO TRAVEL

Well, that was enough for one day. Tonight we would be sleeping in a real bed for the first time since leaving England. Finding your room is no easy task in the size of this hotel. We enter the room, turn the light on, feeling tired we are ready for our sleep. While undressing Steve notices a fly land on the curtains and, getting his shoe, he decides to swat it. One good blow and the whole of the curtains and rail collapse on top of Steve. I was crying with laughter; the largest hotel in the world and he wrecks it. We could be put into a concentration camp. Hurriedly we put it all back together and then slept.

Morning saw us eating black bread, rice, meat, red cabbage and grapes for breakfast. Our first trip this morning took in the art gallery and armoury museum, clothes, coins and weapons, all going back centuries. It is an incredible collection capturing Russia's long and established history. It is like walking down a time tunnel, peering into ancient times and watching progress and advancement that take place through time appear before your very eyes. Outside and in the surrounding area there are massive cannons with balls used many years ago. The river runs slowly around the city, which is enriched with white buildings and churches. On top are the most incredible golden domes and when the sun shines on them they just glisten and shine. It is a very clean city with everything appearing to be well planned and laid out.

We spent the afternoon in Red Square, the seat of power for the whole nation. We were in awe of this area. As you stand facing the Kremlin you see the ledge where all the famous leaders have stood before, Khrushchev, Lenin, Gorbachev, Stalin, and

WHAT A WAY TO TRAVEL

you can imagine a May Day of past years and the passing by of troops, tanks, rockets, guns and missiles that used to parade by. The floor is of cobblestones and they used to be covered to protect the stones from the weight of the machinery. It is said that the surrounding buildings used to shake and rumble as the parade passed. Directly below is Lenin's tomb, with Lenin still lying in state. The public queue for hours to pay their respects to their leader. Story has it that the body was decaying so badly one day while visitors were there an ear fell off. It was now closed for restoration. Behind the stand are the walls of the Kremlin. They are approximately 170 yds long, to the right-hand side is a steeple and on top a huge five-pointed red star. Behind the wall are the Senate buildings and a dome above with a pole and red flag fluttering in the wind. To the left the massive entrance gates with security gates, barriers and armed guards with machine guns. Just to the right is a sentry box manned by armed soldiers. At regular intervals the soldiers leave the box, slow goose-stepping with their guns held in front, straight-armed. They slowly walk the distance of the wall and when they return they relieve the guard and leave the replacement then return the same way. Their feet reach an incredible height and each step their arm comes across their chest. High to the left-hand side is a large clock face and black limousines glide in and out of the iron doors. At one end of the square is the history museum. At the opposite end is St Basil's Cathedral. It has got to be the most decorative and colourful cathedral in the world. It has incredible, beautiful pear-shaped domes and a complementary colour mix. The spires and twisting architecture make it completely unique.

WHAT A WAY TO TRAVEL

A story was told to us as we admired the cathedral. A Czar had requested the architect to design him the best possible cathedral in the world. The result was St Basil's. Pleased with the result, and paying a great deal of money on completion, the Czar asked the architect if he could build an even better cathedral. The architect, being greedy, answered 'Yes', he could, but the Czar had already asked for the best possible so he had his eyes gouged out.

Opposite the Kremlin is Russia's largest shop, which sells most items but would be considered expensive to the locals and slightly drab to the tourists.

The evening we returned to Red Square. By night it is so beautiful and well lit up. The red star shines in the darkness and it is so peaceful.

Our group took in a local bar and joined in the singing. We watched the locals getting plastered, as did our group. Even our guide fell over, drunk. But it was good sharing the night with the locals. Our bar lady, no higher than 5 ft high, gave me a beautiful Russian kiss and hug, kissing either side of my face. On the way home Barry, Steve and I needed to spend a penny. Approaching Red Square we relieved ourselves on the wall, not realising it was part of the Kremlin Wall. As we nearly finished a police car drove past us. We realised how stupid we had been. If we had been caught it would have been seen as an insult to the nation as it was only 50 yds from Lenin's tomb.

After last night's disgraceful behaviour, which must be put down to the strong beer and mixture with 100% proof vodka, we decided that would never happen again as it was such an insult

WHAT A WAY TO TRAVEL

to the country and people, and we wholeheartedly apologise.

On with the tour... The next day saw us taking the Metro. Hans, our guide, told us just how busy this could be. When the train pulls in loads of people will be shoving and pushing to get out and loads shoving and pushing to get in. So he said, 'When I say go, we all move forward together; spread out on the train but stay together. We are only going three stops.' Well, the tube pulled in and the doors opened and they came at us like a steamroller. The men in the group fended them off, protecting the women, then the charge was sounded, 'Go!' and we moved forward like a platoon on the march. We were well pleased with ourselves as the doors closed behind us. All the ladies were safe and unharmed, a bit dishevelled but otherwise ok. Then a shriek of laughter erupted. Everybody was on board except Hans our guide and he was running around frantically.

Our destination was to be a ceiling and it truly is magnificent. Built high up into the domes of an underground station. The ceiling is painted with all types of scenes from aircraft flights from the war to hunting scenes. There are so many to view but it is so beautifully done and in a place you would not normally associate with paintings. The only thing is, it does crick your neck after a while!

We waited for Hans but he never did show up so we carried on with the tour. We visited nearly every landmark there was, and statues. In particular the man and woman holding the hammer and sickle, the symbol of the people, and a huge concrete vapour trail with a rocket on top symbolising their space programme. The libraries and galleries even saw my first

WHAT A WAY TO TRAVEL

painting of the Spanish artist Salvador Dali, and Lenin's statue was in abundance everywhere. We also went shopping although it was difficult to buy souvenir- type items, though I did find a little Russian man doll with hat and boots on. We pinned to him badges we had traded with the children in exchange for sweets, and they had a strange way of paying. Customers would queue and pay, then queue again and wait, and I must admit they were not the friendliest of shop assistants I had come across. However, we did purchase some marvellous stamps of old steam trains although nobody seemed to want our Russian money, roubles. They were quite happy to take our American dollars or any other hard currency.

That evening Barry, Steve and I sat listening to Helena, our tourist guide, singing local folk songs and explaining their stories. She had such a beautiful voice; it was such a pleasure to listen to.

We finished off our last night in Moscow with a small bottle of Russian vodka (I still have the empty bottle) when this well-built blonde Russian lady came over and asked me to dance. 'Never turn a lady down,' I say. We had a great laugh watching each other dance and joining in the local folk dancing. Well, we have experienced a brilliant visit to Moscow, highly recommended, but we have got to keep moving on, back on board the train tomorrow.

Today we joined the Trans-Siberian Express. What an experience this was going to be. Our group was split into two carriages and we were heading for Irkutsk. Trans-Siberian is a magic phrase, which for almost a century has meant only one thing. The world's longest continuous train journey, covering more than 6,000 miles from Europe to the Pacific, and crossing no less than seven time zones. Reaching Siberia it is time to get out our warmer clothes.

En route we passed the Obelisk, marking the passing from Europe to Asia. We are now fully into the swing of being back on a train. The group is even more tightly knitted than before. On board we played Trivial Pursuits, famous quotations, Scrabble, cards, read books, played chess or just sat down or talked, or even just looked out of the window, looking at the countryside or something which caught your eye. Basically just watching the world go by. We had a birthday celebration. Mick, whose birthday it was, supplied the beer. We were sharing with Hans. Every time you walked past their compartment you would hear ZZZST! Another can being opened. Everybody got well happy that night. The chess final was being held between Fred and Hans. I was so sure Fred would win, being a British. Hans challenged me to run the length of the carriage naked if he won.

That night I peeled my clothes off, took a deep, deep breath and, yelling as loud as I could, hands aloft, sprinted as fast as I could. Doors opened along the corridor and a few got a bird's eyes view. Locking the toilet door, I waited for Steve to bring my clothes.

Another funny incident was when we passed through an industrial area. We were advised to keep our windows closed because of soot in the air. Ian, however, found the area fascinating and, with the window open and his head protruding, watched the passing industries. After about five minutes he brought his head inside. His face was black. Not knowing what we were laughing at, he removed his glasses to wipe. He then exploded with laughter. He had these two white circular patches and a black face ,– he looked just like a panda bear. Also, you mix with the local travellers. One little Russian girl called Cecelia was so cute. She was only six years old yet could speak quite a bit of English already, especially songs. In the morning she used to knock our compartment door and sing, 'Good morning, good morning, good morning to you, good morning, good morning, how do you do?' She was lovely. We swapped addresses with her parents and they gave me a Russian record. We taught Cecelia many games such as 'A-tishoo, a-tishoo, we all fall down'. At the end of the train was a no-go carriage. We were told it was the KGB carriage and it seemed they were evident at stations as well. Short sort of stumpy, stocky men in leather jackets, hands in pockets and hats on. And they seemed to watch everybody's movements. There are also lots of military personnel in attendance and at stations.

This time our meals were taken in the restaurant carriage. We were getting used to black bread and soups with everything in them called borscht, and things like orange caviar served by a huge Russian waiter. He looked like a shot-putter. He stood on my foot once! Ouch. Unfortunately I have got chronic diarrhoea. I think it is just the change in water and food diet. The beard is growing nicely, washed my hair in the tiny sink. Not easy. PS Do not forget to bring your own sink plugs!

Irkutsk, Cossack country; this is one of the oldest cities in Siberia. The temperatures can be as low as minus 21 centigrade.

WHAT A WAY TO TRAVEL

The area is very wooded and the houses are one level wooden cabins and a little wooden water well in the garden. In the centre there is a huge plaque in honour of the war dead and it has an eternal flame flickering away. The local school children everyday at regular intervals perform a ceremony of marching slowly around the flame and paying their respects. The final visit in this area is Lake Baikal. It is the deepest and largest natural water lake in the world and it is some 25-30 million years old. It contains more water than the Baltic Sea and with an incredible variety of animal and plant species, three quarters of which are to be found nowhere else on this planet.

On the edge of the lake is a spot where the trees are covered in white pieces of paper or cloth and tissues. It is said that if you place a memento on the tree you will one day return to Lake Baikal. Well, I will just have to wait and see!

We keep moving, through tunnels in the hillside, golden trees on the hillside, picturesque tiny villages, railing sidings with rockets and missiles covered by camouflage netting. Then we notice a temperature change; the cold, chilly wind seems to have eased off Obviously, we are heading south. Within hours the terrain changes to sand. Soon we will be passing through the Gobi desert. It was great when the train eventually stopped and we were able to stand on the sand of the Gobi desert and take photographs. It is completely barren here, and hot. The train moved on. A Russian lady guard walked up to me and asked, 'I sleep with you tonight?' Stunned, I nodded my head. She was extremely attractive, slim with dark hair and a few gold-filled teeth. I told Steve and he was quite shocked. We left it a few

WHAT A WAY TO TRAVEL

hours and then approached her again, asking her what time she would come to the compartment. She pointed to her watch and indicated about twelve midnight. A knock at the door shattered our peace and quiet. I pulled it back and she let herself in, said goodnight, climbed on to the top bunk, faced the wall and went to sleep. Steve and I looked at each other, smirked and got under our own covers and went off to sleep. In the morning she got up early and left. Ah! So that is what she meant, 'I sleep with you,' in broken English. Our excitement over, we watched the train travel through Outer Mongolia, then Inner Mongolia. We were heading for the capital of Mongolia – Ulan Bator. The landscape is of lush green pastures filled with free roaming yaks, a cow-like long-haired bull type and as strong as an ox. The local herdsmen tend their herds on horseback. Their homes are 18-foot-wide tents with a solid door entrance. The stove is the centre point of the room with its funnel extending up through the roof. During the winter months the whole family shares the one single room and stays together for warmth. Their boots and clothing are covered with animal fur. The only thing I never saw was the toilet area; perhaps it just gets too cold. Our group had the opportunity to put on the local gowns, boots and hats and had photographs taken outside the tents, which incidentally are called yurts.

While we were visiting the grasslands and a photograph session with the yaks, hunting men on horseback rode in. Strapped across them were their bows and arrows. We thought that they were going to attack us. It works out they were film extras, as over the next hill a film was being shot, but they looked magnificent in their costumes, riding over the hills.

On to the city. A new and developing city, Ulan Bator has a population of over 400,000 of which 70% are young people less than 35 years of age. The system over here is a family of five children or more is rewarded with a weekly allowance. Big families are encouraged, mainly because it has such a large landscape but is low in population. We found the people here totally fascinating. We spoke to each other in the street, swapping cigarettes, and matches. They talked football and would say Bobby Charlton. On the streets we purchased large pieces of cake for ten pence. We, our clothes, style, way of living fascinates the people but they do not stare or make us feel uncomfortable. In the centre of the city is an incredibly large square. In the centre is a statue of a Mongol on a horse. It is said when the Mongols defeated the Cossacks in a famous battle this is the square that the triumphant Mongols rode to where they announced their famous victory. The statue is a landmark of this particular event.

As we stood there posing for our photographs in that magnificent square we could not help but think back to some of the famous Mongol names that came from this land, Genghis Khan, Kublai Khan and the film portraying the lifestyle of the people, *Taras Bulba* starring Yul Brynner and Tony Curtis. Another visit was to a Buddhist temple, observing the ancient pots and architecture of the building and the dedication of the monks praying, worshipping, singing and chanting. It is a life of devotion dedicated to their beliefs, wearing their orange tunics and shaven heads. They live a simplistic way of life. That evening we visited the local theatre and were treated to a gala performance of music and acrobats contortionists' dance. We saw and heard unique instruments and the notes they played. They sang incredible local folk songs at such pitches and depths. And the music and dance in local costumes was breathtaking and spellbinding. It was a wonderful evening.

The next day we visited the local museum containing bones and structures of ancient dinosaurs found in the surrounding area. On a shopping trip we came across these clay replicas of a man and woman in traditional dress and a tiny ornament of a Buddha, as seen at the temple. These would be my souvenirs. Oh, and moon money. You see, small change is rare so when you purchase an item that requires small change they pay you in sweets or chocolate money. One morning we had shepherd's pie for breakfast, or was it yak meat? I actually lost my appetite here!

We found Mongolia and the people a total fascinating visit. I mean, how many people do you know who have been to Mongolia for a holiday? It made us feel so special but then on this holiday every day has an amazing climax and it just keeps getting better and better.

CHINA

Now we are entering China. As we cross the border we notice a much more relaxed attitude to the passport control we had become used to. You actually felt welcomed as though they wanted you to come visit their country. First job was to change the carriage and wheels back as China used the more conventional

WHAT A WAY TO TRAVEL

system that most of Europe used, and that was it, we were now in China and heading for Peking or, as they say, Beijing. But this was a dream come true. I had always wanted to come here and now I was here. Would it live up to expectations, what will it be like, how will we be treated? Well, read on, because China just blows you away and excels any expectations or ideas and no books you will ever read could do it justice.

As we got off at Beijing station the whole group had a different type of excitement about them. There was an air of anticipation and it starts the moment you first touch the platform. The platform was loaded with crates packed with everything – chickens, pigs, you name it. Chinese men and women running, shouting, arguing. It was a hive of activity. People coming and going and the noise factor, it was like watching organised chaos but it was great to watch and be part of and it really gives you such a buzz.

Outside the station there were thousands of people sitting or squatting on their heels. You see so many people wearing the same sort of clothes, either military in green khaki or civilians in blue trousers and blue jackets. This went for women too, and everybody seems to have thick black hair. At first you think everybody looks identical in features but as you get used to them and study the differences you notice they are all so different and have unique and different faces from eyes, to teeth, lips, body shapes. I only mention this because you pass so many people in a short span of time and, remember, China accounts for 50% of the world's population. We could hardly see any cars but bicycles were in their thousands, or is that millions? Mind

WHAT A WAY TO TRAVEL

you, if everybody had a car the traffic and parking would be horrendous – and the fumes! The coach took us to the hotel. On the way, the group was silent because out of the window there was just so much to look at. Totally mind-boggling. When we reached the hotel we were knocked out, not knowing what to expect. This was five star, doormen, a massive white complex, the reception area had a wall covered in carpet some 150 ft long by 30 ft high. Everything was clean and sparkling. One of the restaurants had its own built-in waterfall and the room was just as spectacular and, of course, a sauna and an indoor pool.

Our first evening, we were being taken to the centre for a traditional meal. Again, the streets were so busy with huge crowds of people. It was explained to us why there were so many. This time of the year is a national holiday, a bit like our Bank Holiday weekend, and everybody was out and about having a good time. I have never seen so many bikes in one place. Everybody seems to have one. At a traffic light the queue of bikes is some ten yds long with more joining every second, and as for the sound of bicycle bells ringing, it really can be quite deafening, but the whole place had a great atmosphere about it. Just to be here is so special. At the restaurant the group was seated at two tables. In the centre was a revolving glass section, then the food arrived and it just kept coming, dish after dish, and plate after plate. In total, thirteen different servings were presented to us. We each had our bowl of rice and put into it anything we chose: pork in batter, vegetables, and bean shoots, meat and mixed combinations. We were later informed that one was snake. When we asked which one, they answered,

'The one that hissed'. The whole atmosphere in the restaurant was marvellous. The waiters were courteous, caring and helpful yet if you wanted to mess about they would join in on the fun. They had a wonderful sense of humour and if you asked for anything, it was never too much trouble. We headed back to the hotel. Steve and I took a swim. Steve had never tried skinny-dipping before so I dared him. After a little coaxing he swam a length and I joined him and really it summed up how we felt, happy, contented, excited, daring, adventurous and free to enjoy it.

FORBIDDEN CITY

The next day our start point was the Forbidden City. Even the name 'Forbidden' conjures up an image. You see, everybody was forbidden entry to this city within a city. This is where the Emperor of China resided. He could not go out and people could not come in. The story is so well captured on film under the title *The Last Emperor*, telling of his childhood years and into manhood, but today we were outside the walls and about to enter. Even the Chinese were fascinated to see inside, something which has been denied them for years, and they came in their droves, some for their very first time.

The walls are huge and very high; they encase the whole city. Entrance is through a small door with a high wooden step so you have to duck and step at the same time. Then you enter into a darkened passageway. There were so many people in this section trying to get through the next door. At the end of the passage after a few minutes of nudging and leaning you are forced through the hole in the wall and catapulted into sunlight.

WHAT A WAY TO TRAVEL

As your eyes adjust there it all is, The Forbidden City, and it is huge. It has ramps, stairways, buildings of all descriptions, wooden sections with door holes where you would go through into the next courtyard. The number 9 was very significant in the structure of the Imperial Palace, for example 9,999 rooms were constructed. There are 9 marbled decorated snakes embedded into an outside wall. The ramps are decorated and patterned. The outhouses were either bedchambers or dining areas. There is a garden area. In abundance there are statues of lions, dragon-type tortoises, birds, metal pots and drums. There are different halls scattered around – the Hall of Jewellery, Hall of Arts and Crafts of the Ming and Qing dynasties, Hall of Ceramics, but my favourite was the Hall of Clocks and Watches.

The Hall of Clocks is so fascinating. They are from all over the world and quite old, and most seem to be in good working order. They were all gifts to the young Emperor. Being as he was young each clock theme is playful; for example, animals would run up ladders and ding bells simulating the chimes. Some were funfair scenes, others magical roundabouts. There were big clock faces or a multitude of faces; they must have been entertaining for the Emperor to watch. And, of course, they were the finest craftsmanship from around the world, not to mention the fine materials used; glass, wood, gold, china – they must be priceless.

After we had been in the Forbidden City for about an hour I turned to Steve, who seemed to be staring into space white-faced as though in shock. I asked him if he was OK and there was no response so I gently shook him. Realising what I was doing he explained that he just could not take all of this in. Not only was it unbelievable to be here but you felt so humble and honoured, also fortunate. I told Steve that is exactly how I felt so let us enjoy it while we can, and we agreed to write diaries to remind us how at certain times we felt and to capture those moments in words.

As we left the encircled walls we stumbled across a street seller who sold tiny replicas of the terracotta army soldiers at Xian. A life-size model was at the hotel, which we posed next to for photographs. This would be a brilliant souvenir to remind us of the day.

But, like I have already said about this holiday, it just keeps getting better. Now we are off to see, to touch and to stand on the Great Wall of China. The only man-made object which is visible from outer space and it is so grand and unbelievable. It just keeps snaking away as far as the eye can see in both directions. And if you manage to get a good viewpoint you can follow its trail into the mountains. Sometimes it disappears from your sight as it winds down the far sides of the hill but reappears and climbs even higher on the next mountain. Now, you have to try and visualise it as it is over 1,200 miles long, almost the length of Britain. It is approximately 18 ft wide and varies in height but averages, say, 20 ft but it goes up and over the most incredible terrain. Mountains, steep cliffs, valleys, dense woodlands and at regular intervals there are watch towers, turrets that climb way above the wall to give vantage look-out points. Also every four feet are slits built into the wall from which you could fire arrows or throw spears or boiling oil. But it allowed the Chinese

WHAT A WAY TO TRAVEL

to defend their territory against the likes of the Moghuls, who used to raid and loot. But when you stand on the wall it is so invigorating, inspiring, awesome. To think this wall was started in the Eastern Zhou Dynasty 770-221 BC, but actually linked together in the third century BC. When you consider the man- and woman-hours of hard labour and toil.

But the biggest mystery of all is where did all the building material come from? In some parts of the region it must have been transported for miles and days at a time. Just to deliver one cartload of blocks, and how was it erected? Consider the steepness of some of the terrain, these are steep mountainsides at incredible angles. They would be hard enough to scale, let along manoeuvre high boulders, but then that's what makes it the Great Wall and why it has got to be classified as a Wonder of the World. When you walk on it, touch it and have your photograph taken on it, it is so special and that is why you have got to come and see it for yourself

We purchased some Chinese peaked hats with dangling medals of the Great Wall and posed for our photographs. In every photograph I seemed so tall, towering over the Chinese people. I am 6 ft 1" but I look like a giant, or was it just the experience that uplifted me? One thing I remember on our section was how steep it was and how slippery it can get, but descending the wall we wanted to get our souvenirs. There is plenty of opportunities as at the bottom there were restaurants and an open market. We purchased these wonderful Chinese rice hats. A beautiful young Chinese lady was sitting on a chair wearing one so Steve and I asked if we could have our photographs taken with her with our new hats on. She obliged and, laughing and giggling all of the time, she gave us the biggest smile on the photographs you will ever see, showing nearly all 32 teeth! Other purchases, a tea towel with the wall and date, a T-shirt stating 'I've climbed the Great Wall of China' in Chinese and English, a gold coin minted of the wall and in a boxed case and a 3 ft x 2 ft rolled poster picture with China at the top, Chinese writing and the Great Wall at the bottom. When I returned home this was framed with a glass front so if I ever want to be reminded of such a stupendous occasion I only have to glance at it.

Oh, and one other thing, my pride and joy, a certificate to commemorate ascending the Great Wall in Beijing with my name on it and date. I got my Chinese guide to sign it as my witness and to write my name in the Chinese language.

Now we were off to visit the Ming tombs. This is an ancient burial place of thirteen previous Emperors. The inside holds the museum pieces and you can watch a short film of the discovery of the tombs. The big door was opened and the expression of the explorer who had discovered them was astonishing. The most fascinating part of the visit for me were the stone animal structures along the roadside leading to the outdoor tombs. These could measure anything from 15 ft high to 20 ft long and the weight must have been incredible. They resembled Chinese warriors in full costume, elephants, and camels kneeling and standing. They cover a distance of over 150 yds, sheltered by trees. It was a pleasant walk down taking in the surrounding scenery.

We headed back towards the centre, stopping at the Chinese

WHAT A WAY TO TRAVEL

Zoo to view the famous black and white pandas. We did not stay long as we had tables booked at a restaurant in the Forbidden City. It looked so different at night all lit up. We walked on the outside of the wall through the gardens. I think everybody was ready for bed, it had been a superb day and we had done and seen so much. Now it was time to rest the body and mind because tomorrow will be just as eventful.

The day began with breakfast in the revolving restaurant on the top floor of the hotel. It allowed you a marvellous aerial view of the city and, with its slow turning motion, the scenery from the window was forever changing. Fred, Steve and I were last to leave. Fred, like myself, liked his cup of tea so we sang to him, 'So Fred and me had another cup of tea and then we went on'. He gave us a great smile and clapped.

First stop today, the Emperor's Summer Palace. This is a huge garden area with its own lake and wooded area. One of the first things you encounter is the long corridor. It must be nearly a mile long but it is so well decorated. Everything had been hand-painted and every 10 feet is an arch and each arch creates a picture or scenery. There are dragons, plants and animals. It must have taken many craftsmen and artists together with numerous visits to complete the corridor. It is well lined with seats and your view would be of the lake. Today paddleboats are used on it. As you emerge through the corridor you catch sight of a life-size paddle steamer, the difference being it is made completely of marble, but its attention to detail is quite unique. Further down is the original first mechanical boat, then you take a twisting and winding path over bridges and through flower

WHAT A WAY TO TRAVEL

gardens. I can imagine in its time that this must have been a very beautiful and peaceful area. Today it is noisy and used as a picnic area.

We had one more visit today but as we passed through the centre it was a hive of activity. Normally the city of Beijing has a population of approximately 9,000,000 people but with people travelling from outside into the centre it seemed as though everybody was on the streets. It was fascinating and Steve and myself wished to be a part of it. So we told the guide that we were cutting our organised tour short, as we wanted to be out there and part of the throbbing crowd and to fend for ourselves. She gave us 6 hours to mingle. It felt strange to part from our group and was the first time any of us had been parted but this was too good to miss and we just wanted to mingle.

We headed for Tiananmen Square. On a normal day you would get no more than a couple of hundred people walking across it at one time, going about their business. Today it was shoulder to shoulder and packed solid, and this is a huge square. It is probably equivalent to eight football pitches and there was not a spare inch. When in the crowd you found a line that moved forward and just joined it and at a snail's pace shuffled forward. We headed for the centre where there was a type of platform, a vantage viewpoint. Once up there we had an incredible view. Around the edges are the political buildings and at the far end the Memorial Hall of Chairman Mao. Just off the centre was a 15 ft high and 30 ft long dragon made of flowers and its head actually moved from side to side, and that is what we headed for. All around us everybody was happy and laughing and

WHAT A WAY TO TRAVEL

taking photographs. It was a superb atmosphere. We reached the dragon and used that as our backdrop for our photographs. Next destination the Memorial Hall. Now, in a crowd like this going forward is OK but if you wish to change direction and walk sideways it is not at all easy. You hit oncoming pedestrians and if you slow down or stop to give way then you get bumped and trodden on from behind, but made it we did. The building had a red tiled roof and a large picture of Chairman Mao on the facing wall.

We did not go inside because of the queues but we were told his embalmed body was on display inside. Outside on the building many red flags were flying and the front portion of the road was fenced off just for bicycles, and there were thousands of them. We got a good photograph standing next to a stone lion with the Memorial Hall behind, along with a picture of Chairman Mao.

To the left of the building an archway took us into the gardens. It was pleasant just to rest for a while. Here we met many students who went out of their way to talk to us. One group of about ten mixed students wanted to know everything about the Western way of life and our own perceptions of Asia and China, and we longed to hear about their views on the West. They thought we went to discos every night. They wanted to know about girlfriends and how many different women I had slept with. After I told them, I asked about their love lives. They answered that it was unusual to have sex before marriage and the authorities penalised families with more than one child. So it was important to find your lifelong partner in case a mishap

WHAT A WAY TO TRAVEL

occurred and you might not have a child with your selective partner. They wanted things from the West so badly. Freedom to move around was one, and being allowed to travel abroad. Freedom of press and freedom of speech, and they predicted there would be an uprising of the students in protest, and for progress. We had an incredible hour of conversation with the group exchanging ideas, theories and our totally different way of life and politics. When the recent problems occurred in Tiananmen Square I thought of the students we had met and hoped that they were all safe. I was not surprised that it had happened as the students had predicted it would. We parted company. They had given us directions to local shops and an open market and that is what we headed for as it was time to shop for souvenirs.

Our guide had taught us a few little Chinese sayings, e.g. Hello - Ne-How; How much? - Door-Sow-Chang?; I love you - Wae-Eye-Knee; Thank you - Chey-Chey. Well, that is very roughly how you would pronounce the words. You have to remember there are two different dialects here, Mandarin and Cantonese, and one written word can be used in three different tones, low, medium and high, so you could use the wrong one and be totally misunderstood. Anyway, Steve wished to buy an item on the top shelf of a floor cabinet. It had no price on it. Steve was struggling with communication so I stepped in with my perfect Chinese. Door-Sow-Chang? At the right pitch. The shop assistant understood perfectly and came back with her answer, of which I could not make head or tail. Steve asked me, 'How much?' I told him the price and once he had sorted his money he gave it to her. She wrapped the item and they exchanged Chey-Cheys. Steve looked at me and asked, 'How did you know what she said?' 'Easily,' I replied, 'If you had looked in the cabinet on the shelf below it had the same item but with the price clearly displayed.' We fell about laughing which in turn made the young shop assistants start to laugh with us.

I love this type of shopping. Everything is so different you can look at the local arts and crafts, the colours used, the materials, the great detail and stickers which say 'Made in China'. Now we foreigners to China exchange our money when we enter the country and we are given our own money. They are called Foreign Exchange Certificates but sometimes in the change you are given the local money. As we shopped we purchased many items: a real china teapot and a cup with a lid on decorated in blue ink of dragons, a silk pin cushion with a Chinese dance lady printed on it and around the outside twelve little Chinaman heads, a green dragon, a plastic snake toy which walked across the floor, a little old Chinese lady and a bald man whose heads were on springs and wobbled when touched, a golden ornament pot, postcards of scenery and golden book markers with Chinese writing and my favourite, a Chinese doll wearing the straw hats we had purchased earlier in very simply clothing and shoes, long black silky hair and carrying a basket on her arm.

We also visited the market and took in the sights and sounds. Time was getting on and we had to be at our meeting point by 6 p.m. Having no maps or no clue where it was we stopped an old man on a bicycle taxi. A push bike front with two seats at the rear over each wheel. We showed him the address and he knew where it was and off we went. It was great being part of the cyclists. We stopped when they did. They overtook us on the inside and out. There are all walks of life on the bikes, young, old, families with children. We were on the bike for about 15 minutes and we gave him a good tip. He posed with us and his bike for the customary photographs.

Well, he had delivered us right outside the Peking Duck restaurant. It was not long before the group joined us. They were all eager to learn what we had been up to. We had all our stories to tell but we also wanted to know what we had missed. When we parted company they got stuck in heavy traffic. Shame. Visited a circular thing, which was boring. Ah, shame. Went back to the hotel in long traffic jams. Ah, shame. Slept, washed and changed, rejoined the lengthy traffic jams and came here. Ah, shame.

Whereas we had one of the best afternoons of our lives. Inside the restaurant was beautifully decorated. Free beer was supplied followed by clear mushroom soup and then the world famous duck. Using your paper thin pancake wrappings you spread the brown sweet sauce over your pancake, sprinkle it with delicious tender duck meat and munch away. Repeat until full. Exhausted, we reached the hotel. Steve and I decided to get a couple of beers, return to our room, watch a bit of television and write our postcards home. They went something like this: -

'Broke through the Berlin Wall, escaped the KGB,
walked across the Gobi desert, climbed the Great Wall
of China and it won't be long B4 we're in Hong Kong'

WHAT A WAY TO TRAVEL

Well, today we leave Beijing with nothing but happy memories. The people are so friendly and kind, the place fascinating to explore. We decided this is more than just a holiday, it is an adventure, a spectacle on life and different ways of living. It is an education and proves the saying 'Travel broadens your mind and opinions on life situations'.

Back on the train, we are moving deep south heading for Canton. We will be travelling through the heart of China seeing the small villages, the crops in the fields, especially the rice fields, which are filled with water and tea plantations. These are hardworking farmers who help feed the vast population. You can watch the oxen in the fields working, the horse and carts carrying supplies.

As we travelled down we crossed the Yangtze River. Here the temperature totally changed into hot and humid conditions.

But it is the chance meetings on trains with people that can change your life forever. The first person who stands out is Nog, a Norwegian lady, a solo traveller. Our meeting took place in our train compartment.

Cecelia burst through the door, sat down and said, 'OK guys, abuse me.' She did not mean physically but verbally. She had short-cropped, naturally blonde hair, an extremely pretty face and a well-endowed body. Quite sumptuous, I would say. For two hours she told us stories, about herself, her home life, why and how long she had been travelling. We told our stories and jokes and everybody enjoyed himself or herself. Nog and I kept in touch for years. We wrote letters, back and forth all around the world. She even came to visit me in England and she still refers to me as 'Brown Eye' because when I stood up to get something down from the racks, Barry pulled my pants mooning Nog two feet from her face. Hence 'Brown Eye'. She told me one day she would write a book about her travels and I would be in it. Well, Nog, I have already done it and you are part of it.

At one station as people were getting on the train, Steve and I were in the corridor. A Chinese lady got on wearing a light green top; one could not help but notice her protruding large breasts. Having not seen too many well-developed ladies in China I could not help but mention it to Steve out loud verbally. The lady disappeared up the corridor with her case to the end compartment. She put her case in, then returned to where we were standing. In the most soft, quiet and well-spoken English she asked, 'Do you speak English?' From that moment I was smitten and fell in love instantly. She had long, strong black hair with a beautiful smiling face and the cutest of eyes I have ever seen. Her movements and poses were so delicate and precise and her laughter was infectious. I asked her name. Ching Ching. It sort of sang at me. Ching Ching. We were inseparable for two days. We taught her new words, showed her how to play 'Snap' with cards and just had the most romantic time I can ever remember. She was so charming and cute. Her English was very good but sometimes she struggled for words, but that added to her charm and charisma. I will never forget our first kiss; it was so tender and passionate. Ching Ching and I communicated together for years to come with some of the most fantastic letters I will ever receive. We frequently telephoned each other and while she was in Italy studying Italian I stayed with her for

WHAT A WAY TO TRAVEL

three months, but the parting on the train was oh, so painful.

On this leg of the journey Barry, Fred, Steve and I shared a compartment. To us it just added to the fun. They were great company. We played card games, drank tea and beer, generally having a good time. This train was of a lower standard than we had got used to. We tried the restaurant carriage a few times but generally gave it a wide berth. Barry had videoed most of the holiday so when the little girl from next door came into our carriage Barry put her on video. She was only four and a half years old. She was so cute and could already recite the English alphabet and count to ten. When she saw herself on playback on the video she was amazed. We gave her a little clinging teddy bear and she loved it. In the mornings Fred and I used to sing to Steve to get him out of bed. One particular morning, however, we did not need to. Once I told him there was a huge cockroach walking up the wall right near his head he was up and out like a shot, and I was not kidding.

We arrived in Canton and transferred to the hotel. It was another superb quality hotel. Steve and I were last to check in. Unfortunately there was no room for us. Everybody disappeared to unpack, wash, change and get ready for the city tour. We, however, sat on the sofa and were treated to a beer for our troubles. By the time a room became available the tour had left so we decided to walk to the local market. We found Sue lurking in the foyer. She had missed the tour as well so we invited her to join us.

The market was fascinating. It sold everything, and I mean everything. There are things on sale you would not find anywhere else in the world. For example, all types of birds, fish, bears' paws, cats, chickens, terrapins, pigeons, guinea pigs, ducks, snakes, eels, badgers and weasels, and most were alive. Not to be kept as pets but to be eaten. There were also huge sacks of tobacco and they rolled you a cigarette and you smoke them before choosing. Boy, they were strong. But this really was an eye-opener into the Chinese way of life. This was further endorsed when we walked back through the park and watched the young and old exercise with their unique movements. Spinning and turning on one foot, arms circulating in slow motion. Back to the hotel we decided to take a tour of the hotel. It had superb shopping facilities, silk gowns, arts and crafts, jewellery and a beautiful carved ship from wood. Tonight we were taken for a traditional Cantonese meal. On the way home on the coach I treated everybody to a song. Once in a while you won't call but it's all in the game. The game called love. The group cheered and whistled, even my brother said he could not believe it. He said he did not know that I had such a good voice. One lady said I sounded just like Cliff. My head was getting big until I was told not to give up my day job!

Today we are leaving China. We have had a superb time. Fantastic memories, and we have met some super people and hopefully lifetime friends. Today we will be passing through the new territories by train and getting off at Kowloon Island then to be transferred to Hong Kong islands by ferry. Our group had become one big happy family and it is decided to have a farewell party in Hong Kong. After our visit here people will be going in every direction, some to Australia, New Zealand, some to visit Japan, others are staying on in China and taking a tour. One couple is going to Korea and some are going straight home to England. We had already booked an extension for two days in Hong Kong.

HONG KONG

In 1997 this island will be given back to the People's Republic of China so we wanted to see it as it was before the changes take place and, believe me, there is so much here to see and enjoy.

I remember approaching by train and seeing the border lined by fences, barbed wire and watchtowers. We wondered what would be the 'must visit' points. My vision of Hong Kong was as a child, nearly every toy you had was stamped or marked with the words 'Made in Hong Kong', so my imagination was a city filled with toy factories and warehouses of toys, as we entered immigration and transferred by ferry to the islands.

The last sight I expected was a bay full of towering skyscrapers. As we travelled through the centre to our hotel the streets were alive and bustling with shoppers and suited office workers. It was packed with people going this way and that and at the typically fast pace of any city. Every shop seemed to have a marked sign outside of it, some even reached from one side of the street to the other. We booked into a marvellous hotel but could not wait to hit the streets to feel the atmosphere and be part of the bargain shopping capital of the world. It seemed to sell everything and the prices seemed very competitive. We went on a shopping spree. We could not resist the colours, the novelties and, most of all, a good bargain. My first purchase was

WHAT A WAY TO TRAVEL

a wristwatch with a difference. The background was a spider's web with two standard hands but a spider constantly chasing as the seconds tick by., T-shirts with all types of motifs, a lighter with a case cover with Hong Kong printed on it, a beautiful ancient junk, a silk red kimono with a colourful dragon design on the back and our usual doll with a beautiful head piece silk dress and opened red fan draped over her arm, plus stacks of colourful postcards.

But the streets were amazing, a hive of activity, it seemed every three paces you could get something to eat, sweet, sour, burned, fresh or cooked openly. You could get an abundance of seafood and most of it was alive, swimming or crawling around in front of you, crab, lobster, crayfish, oysters, prawns, snakes, eels. It seemed if it moved they caught it and sold it. And what was hanging on hooks above the counter had either been squashed, flattened, pickled, steamed or simply left to the elements, and that included dust and exhaust fumes, but it was all fascinating whether you were buying or just looking. We also could not resist jumping the local trams. There were so many running and each decorated so well. Bright colours or used for advertising, slogans, usually you wait an hour then three come along. Here you get three every minute.

When we arrived at the harbour, a trip had been organised on a motorised junk. What a way to see the area from the waterline. There are people living on the junks who have never stepped foot on Hong Kong soil. Children who have never set foot on land. They are prohibited and if they set foot ashore they would be arrested. Some junks are falling apart, some are seaworthy, and others are like factories, processing all types of seafood. On many junks washing lines are filled with fish drying. The entire family seem to participate. Little boats shuttle from junk to junk, servicing and supplying everything including drinking water. The centrepiece of the harbour has just got to be the floating restaurant, Jumbo and Shatin. It is said that the food is fantastic and at night when the restaurant is all lit up it actually glows in the darkness and reflects in the water. The lights take the shape of a palace; very picturesque yet the other side of the water there is so much poverty and deterioration.

As we took in the sights, sounds and smells and believe me the water can get a bit pongy and stagnant and with the put put put of our engine, it dawned on me just how far away from home we were!

Next stop the jewellery factory, watching the rings, brooches and necklaces being made, displayed and sold. Too much for me to pay. That was the end of our city tour but this evening we were to go downtown to the red light district known as WAN CHAI. It certainly opens you eyes, topless bars, film shows, ladies of the night openly walking on the street, massage parlours and game rooms for the old men who play the dice game Mahjong. We also noticed a few undesirables hit the street as it got later. Men and women begging, some looked completely down and out. We left the area and went to see a floodlit football match. At midnight a street market develops along a side street. This really was bargain time, mainly for the locals but tourists were just as welcome. It was marvellous watching the street come alive with colour and people bartering for their goods. Well,

WHAT A WAY TO TRAVEL

they say everything must come to an end and this was the end of this holiday. Adventure, and what a time we have had and what a way to travel! What memories.

The last leg of the journey took us back via Dubai. Unfortunately the aeroplane broke down at the airport so we had to change planes. We let everybody go first, which worked for our good fortune as the only seats left were in first class. The only problem was we had to do an emergency landing at Rome airport where the aeroplane was fixed on the tarmac. What with the two delays, detour, loading and unloading, generally waiting around, the flight home from Hong Kong to London took 35 hours but after the trip we had just had we had no complaints.

AROUND THE WORLD IN 28 DAYS

STOPPING AT USA - LOS ANGELES, MEXICO, HAWAII - HONOLULU, NEW ZEALAND - AUCKLAND, AUSTRALIA - SYDNEY, THAILAND BANGKOK, PATTAYA (VIA INDIA), LONDON

Our flight path to Los Angeles, United States of America, took us over Iceland, Greenland and Canada. It was a magical bonus to fly over these lands. What with being such a clear day our view and photographs are marvellous. You can see in great detail a landscape of snow, mountains, crevices and valleys. It would appear to be a terrain that would be difficult to cross and I wondered if this was probably the best way in which to see the landscapes by flying directly over.

Over Canada, parts of the NorthWest territories, then the Rocky Mountain range before descending into LA.

Although brother Steve and I had been to LA before, each travel experience picks out different memories. I guess because you are in a different time and places so the people and characters you meet change, which of course leads to distinct incidents, and there is always something new or different or something you missed the first time round. For example, our hotel was the Hollywood Roosevelt Hotel. The Blossom Room was the site of the First Academy Awards presentation presided over by Douglas Fairbanks. Oscars were given out and it is recorded that such stars as Clark Gable, Carole Lombard, Errol Flynn and David Niven either visited or stayed at this hotel. The balcony above has loads of memorabilia of stars and their films. In the foyer is a bronze statue sitting on a bench with his bowler hat, boots and cane, arms crossed, with his tie on and the wrinkled jacket of Charlie Chaplin. So I sat next to him and had my photograph taken with one of my all-time favourites of film. Across the road was the Chinese Theatre with the landmarks in cement. This time, however, we had more time to look at all the star prints and plaques and we could go and see them at any time. Steve had never been to Mexico but the bonus was he would be going into Seaworld. Our Chinese driver was great fun and he knew all the best places to visit in our whistle- stop tour. Watching the dolphin and whale shows is fantastic and a real thrill. There was a pirate ship and a show including sea lions, seals and big old walrus. Then there is the shark tank and all other sea creatures, which can be viewed through the glass. I find it fascinating watching them glide through the water going about their business. Mexico: Tijuna had the same feel about it for me but Steve enjoyed the experience, especially the two little Mexican dolls he purchased. The rest of the time in LA we just window-shopped, got used to the jet lag, took an early night and basically prepared ourselves for tomorrow's adventure. We were off to our dream place, the islands of Hawaii.

WHAT A WAY TO TRAVEL

HAWAII - HONOLULU

The first thing that struck me was the warmth and not just of the sun but of the people. After travelling far and wide you would have to go a long way to find people so warm and friendly. After learning the local greeting of 'Aloha' you really learn how to smile here. It is infectious. Upon our arrival we had placed around our necks a closely knitted ring of flowers. The odour was sweet and the flowers colourful and soft. As we stood in our magnificent hotel room we knew this was one of those places you love and could not help but enjoy the whole place. The hotel had its own channel on information and tourist travel and visits. It was very informative and helped us to plan and organise our trips, seeing as much as possible in a limited time.

First on our list – the shopping arcades. Open markets. It is a great way to meet the local people and converse with them. The shop stalls had so much colour on them, shells of all shapes and sizes, jewellery, bright colourful shirts, dolls, imitation silk flowered necklaces, shields, boats and pictures. The storekeepers were so very friendly. We purchased silk necklaces, Hawaiian dancing dolls, shells and colourful Hawaiian shirts and now we were ready for the beach. Not just any old stretch of sand but the world famous – and certainly known throughout the world – Waikiki Beach. Set into a beautiful bay with hills as the backdrop, bright white clean sand, light warm sky blue, clear sea, it is a beach bather's paradise. It is also an action-packed setting along with all types of watersports. It is a surfer's paradise, incredible rolling breaking waves, and white surf. There are all types of boat trips, which you can take from the shoreline. There are the paddle canoeing catamarans, the family size rowing boats, and speedboats. You can just lie there and watch all the activity take place or you can get up and participate, but if neither of these appeal to you then you can turn to your neighbour on the beach and speak to people from all parts of the world. Failing this just sit and watch or look at some of the most beautiful girls in the world, and girls, the men look all right too. And you will see some of the skimpiest bathing suits you will ever see and everybody seems to have a golden bronzed tan.

Well, having tasted and tested the beach and sea, it was time to explore. We booked a snorkelling course at Hanauma Bay; the drive through the hills gave us a flavour of the country. Deep green plantation, flowers in abundance, tropical-like plants, palm trees gently blowing in the breeze. We passed Tony Curtis's home (the actor), then arrived at this most picturesque bay. At the far end the hills almost touched each other. The sand was golden and the water clear blue and green. It was quite a way down the steps to the beach but it seemed a fun place to be. We were given our lessons on how to breathe through the snorkel pipe and told that the first part of the sea was filled with rocks so once you had your flippers on your feet it was best to walk backwards into the sea, as it gave you a better balance and stopped the flippers getting trapped on the rocks. Armed with our bag of green peas and a handful of bread we walked backwards into the sea. What a sight we looked. Steve and I were laughing our heads off, watching each other as we stumbled over the rocks with a big pair of goggles on, breathing out of a tube. With great big flippers on, walking backwards,

WHAT A WAY TO TRAVEL

falling everywhere and carrying bread and peas. Peas, you may ask? According to our instructor the fish love to eat the peas, they go mad for them and, of course, if you feed the fish more will gather around you and you can get a good view of them while they feed.

Well, we eventually got into the water up to about our hips. The bottom of the seabed was now soft sand and the sea was warm. Steve was about six feet in front of me, wading out with his arms above water, swinging from side to side. Lifting your feet with those damn flippers and placing them down is not easy. I, for some reason, lowered my hands into the water not realising there were so many fish already around me. They swarmed at me to get the food. I totally panicked and jumped with fright. These were large fish. Losing my balance and falling backwards I threw my bread upward to get the fish away from me. Unfortunately it landed within two inches of Steve's black swimming trunks. Now, imagine poor Steve. Right at his backside were fish nibbling away. He panicked as well and threw his bread in my direction. By now I was in the water, floating on my back. When the bread landed and the fish arrived I just threw everything up in the air, especially the peas. I have never seen it rain peas before but as they hit the water they were swallowed up. Steve and I just stood there crying with laughter, so much so, we had to take our goggles off and pipe out. But what topped it off was an old American lady with a large black baggy swimsuit saying to us, 'You two are crazy, I'm getting out of here.' We just burst; we could even see people on the beach laughing at our antics.

WHAT A WAY TO TRAVEL

So we replaced our bits and submerged and it is the most wonderful thing you can do. Being part of the sea and watching nature. The fish are superbly coloured, all shapes and sizes, graceful in their movements and they are pure magic to watch. It is as if every fish has its own character. Some are curious, some mischievous, some lazy, some uncaring and we loved every moment of it. One word of caution: you forget the sun is belting down on parts of your body above water so it is a good idea to cover your shoulders or at least protect your back with suncream.

We had a fantastic day but it was not over just yet. We got back to our room, showered and shaved. Put on our new colourful Hawaiian shirts, our silk flowers around our neck, a pair of shorts; flip-flops on, we were going out to something the locals called Luau. The fun starts as soon as you get on the coach. Our guide was a laugh a second. He told jokes and stories. We sang songs. He even taught us some Hawaiian words such as Near Bush. Then he points in the distance and says Far Bush!

He also taught us the hand greeting. Hold your hand up in the air, close the middle three fingers and shake both hands back and forth like a semi-circle and say the word 'Aloha'! And when you overtake another coach on the way to the Luau you either pretend you're all asleep or stick your tongue out with your thumb on your nose and wiggling your fingers. Or everybody has to look the other way. A couple of times we all pretended to be rowing in a boat. The funny thing is all the other coaches are all doing the same thing. It is a real laugh and really sets you up for what is to come.

WHAT A WAY TO TRAVEL

Once the coach stops you are confronted with a huge wooden fence. The entrance is through large wooden gates and above the gate is a sign stating Paradise Cove – and they are not kidding. As you enter you are given two free drinks, a Hawaiian blue cocktail and a Tia Maria punch. There are beautiful ladies waiting to greet you with their long, black, silky hair, grass skirts and two coconut shells as a bra, and they are prepared to pose with you while you have your photograph taken. My lady was extremely cute, slim, a smashing smile and wide awake eyes. As I put my arm round her, I felt her silky hair brush over my arm. I felt as though I could marry her on the spot, or at least take her home. Later when the photograph was developed I popped back to see her and asked her to sign her name. Not only did she sign but she also kissed me. I will never wash my face again!

Inside everything is happening. There are local and ancient games to play, for example, there is an old straw target which you throw spears at. Also a type of bowling alley. The balls are small stone boulders. Both Steve and myself hit the required amount down. Our reward, a shell-made necklace. It is my pride and joy. There are men in local traditional dress climbing straight up coconut trees, bare foot and no supports. They shower down flower petals and it is said if you catch one you will return to Hawaii and get married. Then you are taken to the beach, a beautiful sandy cove with the sea gently sloshing onto the sand. A shell conch is blown, an ear-piercing horn. Men appear with fishing nets and throw them into the sea to catch our fish for the evening meal. Earlier pigs had been wrapped in leaves and lowered into the sandpits. The ground covers hot molten

WHAT A WAY TO TRAVEL

lava, which steams the pigs. The King and Queen perform a ceremony. We all give our thanks for the food we are about to eat, and then it is taken away and cut up. You are served the tenderest delicious pork you have ever tasted accompanied with jacket potatoes and salad. You sit at long tables and meet your fellow party makers and as you eat and drink the sun sets over the cove. It is so romantic, then you are treated to another feast. A feast of entertainment, Hawaiian music, singing, dancing, fire eating acts and dancing. Then the acts disappear and you can go on stage and dance to your heart's content. All done under the bright moon and these quaint little night lights. What an evening of fun, games, good food and entertainment. And those dancing Hawaiian girls with their hips bouncing in and out – what a night. And there was still the fun to come on the way home on the coach. That night in bed with my shell necklace around my neck and clutching my souvenir photograph I fell into a deep dream.

The morning started with a fresh fruit breakfast. Today we wanted to pay a respectful visit to Pearl Harbour, the site of the Japanese attack, which brought America into the Second World War. We first visited the war museum, which gives the background to that fatal day. It was a Sunday morning on 7th December 1941. A Navy not at war had some 95 ships moored around Ford Islands. The Japanese launched a massive air attack, some 353 aeroplanes at 7.55 a.m. The first enemy planes appeared overhead. Photographs, film and memorabilia, war medals, photographs and letters written by sailors and sent home, display what happened next.

WHAT A WAY TO TRAVEL

There is also a memorial to the ship US Arizona which took a direct hit and sank very quickly, entombing all 1,177 crew members. The ship is still visible under the water from the White Bridge platform placed across its bows. It is said that oil still leaks from her, which is clearly visible. You take a short boat ride out to the memorial. It was strange to see so many Japanese paying their respects but very brave, admirable and respectful. They would drop flowers onto the water but you could still feel the tension on that spot between Americans and the Japanese. Just showing that war scars can take a long time to heal but standing there, thinking of all of those young men who had lost their lives and the suffering of the families involved, made you feel sad and distressed. One other thing I noticed was a framed glass picture of the Admiral who led the Japanese fleet. The glass had been severely scratched across the face area, showing still how people are affected by the day's event.

On our way back we stopped at the Old Palace. Out the back garden a Hawaiian wedding was taking place. Our last stop was the war cemetery, the sight of an old volcano. Hawaii is notorious for its active volcanoes and the hotel tourist channel gives a good showing of the many molten liquid lava flows.

The last evening we wanted to celebrate. This is such a unique place we just wanted to give thanks. One hotel we visited had a huge aquarium tank and there were all types of sea creatures to view while you have a drink. Even late at night the market stalls are open for trade and in one shopping precinct we watched the Hula girls dancing once more to magical Hawaiian music, and in the background a cascading waterfall.

WHAT A WAY TO TRAVEL

What a place, what a visit and what fantastic and lovely people. Some of my memories, the five Hawaiian ladies with their grass skirts, flower head pieces and necklaces holding up the letters spelling HAWAII, me standing under a banner doing the Hawaiian hand welcome with the words on it WELCOME TO HAWAII A1 STAR, dancing with my flowers on in the hotel room, the picture with the two coconuts, the shopping mall with the dancers kissing Steve, the postcards of the flowers, Waikiki Beach, the surfers, the sun setting over this marvellous country. I love Hawaii. Aloha, I will be back. Meanwhile I have always got my gloss-framed picture of palm trees and the sun setting behind them to remind me and help me dream about my return.

NEW ZEALAND - AUCKLAND

Today's flight to New Zealand was very special, as we would be flying over the International Date Line. It is like losing a complete day. We were 12 hours behind the UK and within one second we were 12 hours ahead. As we arrived at the airport we noticed our first drops of rain.

Now this is the land of 3 million people and 50 million sheep. We checked into our super hotel. This was so high-class. Princess Anne had got the whole of the 9th floor and was staying there during our visit. That evening as we walked out of the hotel great big black limousines were pulling up and well-dressed ladies and gentlemen emerged. By all accounts there was to be a function here tonight and Princess Anne was to be guest of honour. We strolled around the hotel to the back door. We stood there for a minute when a Range Rover pulled up and

WHAT A WAY TO TRAVEL

guess who got out, no other than the Princess herself and she was dressed in her riding gear. She opened the boot of her car, took some items out and she was only about six feet away from us. Then she went into the hotel. It is not every day you get that close to a member of the Royal Family. On another occasion we pressed the 9th floor button in the lift just to see if it would go up there. We thought for security reasons it would not go up there but to our amazement the doors opened on nine. We stumbled out of the lift, the startled receptionist looked at us shocked and security guards moved towards us. We apologised, got back into the lift and got out of there, but I did laugh when Steve said, 'Well, I can tell all of my friends back home I've slept in a bed under the same roof as a Princess.'

That night we had a pizza and ended up around the dock area watching the ships coming and going in the night. We were a little messed up at that moment, what with the time difference, so decided on an early night as tomorrow looks quite an action-packed and busy day.

First stop today – Mount Eden, an old dormant volcano high up in the hills surrounding Auckland's harbour. Fantastic view of the surrounding area. Auckland is called the City of Sails and from our high vantage point you can see why. It is said there are over 50,000 yachts and boats in the harbour, and what a spectacular and colourful scene they make. Little white sails fluttering in the wind. Took a marvellous photograph of me with the harbour and city in the background, a map of the area with the sign above showing 'Maungawhau Domain the Maori Influence'.

WHAT A WAY TO TRAVEL

Our next port of call – Kelly's Waterworld. Now to get to this we had to cross the Nippon Clip-on Bridge, so named because it was designed and manufactured in Japan and it just clips onto the original structure, hence the name. Well so our guide said, anyway. I think he was pulling our legs, but we all laughed anyway.

Kelly's Waterworld is fantastic. The layout inside is incredible. The design is of see-through plastic tubing so this is the area you would walk through. Above you and to the sides are the marine life separated into different sections where there are all types of sea creatures. A variation of sharks, the majestic sting rays, but what makes it so unique is how close you feel to them. They glide, float and swim over you, beside you and around you. You can get an incredible view of the underside of a shark or the sting ray as it glides by above you or eye-to-eye contact as it swims at you then diverts away at the last second. In the souvenir sections there are these wonderful boards with pictures of sharks on together with male and female divers with cut-outs to place your own head. They make for brilliant photographs. There is even one with a diver being cuddled by an octopus.

Our next stop was the exhibition centre and museum. Being this was a Sunday and, incidentally, Anzac Day, when we arrived at the State House a full military parade was taking place with the marching bands and previous military personnel in attendance, paying their respects to the dead, wounded and survivors of the 1st and 2nd World Wars.

After lunch we were at leisure for the rest of the day. Steve and I checked out the main shopping area. It is a great place to talk and mingle with the locals. It seems a very clean city although it does have its naughty section with walk-in and view video shops and bars, but tonight we have decided on getting a few beer cans, watching a film on television and getting our diaries up to date. So we went into this sort of wine shop, looked around but could not see any beer cans so we asked the shopkeeper, 'Do you sell beer?' The answer came back with his accent on it, 'Na mate, it's against the law, but I've got some out the back if you want them?' It creased us up and typified their sense of humour and fun.

Up early this morning as we have got a long drive right through the countryside and landscape to visit Rotorua, a Maori village. First stop en route was a sheep shearing station. Try saying that after a drink. We had a great visit here to see so many breeds of sheep. I though once you had seen one sheep you had seen them all. Wrong. There are all shapes and sizes, horned, woolly-haired, different colour shades, but most surprising of all are they have a terrific character. Some even opened latch gates to get to the food but they did look splendid, each standing on their own breed type plate. Next we watched a sheep being sheared. It is completed so quickly; the poor little sheep are left naked and skinny.

Outside a show was put on showing the sheep dogs rounding the sheep up and penning them. Also on the grounds was a huge stone statue of a bird. It was some 18-foot high, its legs were so long, and all 6 foot of me could stand under its body reaching my arms up. It looks as though I am carrying the whole structure with its scaly body and 6-foot-long neck. It looks prehistoric. Across the road is a unique zoo. You walk through a type of rain forest where you can view the habitat of the kiwi bird unique only to New Zealand. There are a few huts showing the bird in detail including its eggs. Inside the darkened hut are a few of the Kiwis. On the grounds outside is a collection of local exotic birds and streams holding the rainbow trout.

Just down the road we enter the Maori Village of Rotorua. After being shown local craftsman chiselling wood into boats, masks and ornaments we are treated to the Powhiri, a traditional welcome.

The Maori men and women all in their traditional dress of skirts, head pieces and pom poms do a conventional welcome dance. It is a very active dance with added pieces like the protruding flicking tongue and the rubbing of noses. Also the singing and chanting make it a very special event. Not to mention the colourfully decorated faces and bodies. A fortified Maori village called A (Pa) covers the area, a Maori tribe still lives in the Whakarewarewa Reserve. We were taken to the surrounding area which displays boiling mud, bubbling away, erupting geysers, shooting and spraying water way up into the air, colourful silica deposits and hot springs steaming sulphur which you can smell in the air, a geothermal Pandora's Box. It was amazing walking across this bridge with the geysers, sulphur and boiling mud. It is like being on another planet.

Outside one of the traditional homes, Steve and I posed for our usual photographs but leaning against the centre pole we decided to stick our tongues out. Not quite as good as the postcards we purchased with the Maori men doing it, but it does look funny. Also we found the people really charming and caring. Our local Maori guide was fantastic at explaining things and the way of her people. I asked if she would pose with me on a photograph. 'Yes,' she answered, and took me to the white entrance arch. Putting our arms around each other it made for a great snap, with the word Te Hokowhitu-a-Tu arched above us. We also purchased some super souvenirs from here: Maori black dolls decorated in feathers showing the traditional costumes, a tiny silver kiwi bird and a plastic cocktail stick with a kiwi bird on top, an Air New Zealand sticker and a rugby All Blacks sticker.

This has been a very informative visit, a great adventure. It has been terrific seeing another way of life and a different culture. The people have been very kind with a good sense of humour and I do not think you could get much further from home if you tried, yet it seems as though you are at home with its similarities and customs and general way of life and fashions.

AUSTRALIA - SYDNEY/MELBOURNE
(GOOD DAY, MATE)
Through my life in films, documentaries and news bulletins together with photographs, paintings and even postcards I have seen the Sydney Opera House, and the more I got to view it the more I wanted to view it for myself To actually be there – and today that dream would come true.

After booking into the hotel and dumping our cases we headed straight for it and it is as splendid as I ever thought it would be.

WHAT A WAY TO TRAVEL

The design of the structure is totally superb and unique and, something I had never realised from photographs or films, it is also so practical. For one thing, I thought it was one building with sections. It is actually sections that look like one building. The height was the next shock as it is massive and each dome has a glass filling. It seems to have ten orange type segments facing upwards but different viewing angles give you a distinct impression. From straight on it looks like two rows increasing in size from front to back, and from the side they seem to face every which way.

But I was here to touch it. I wanted to feel it so that every time it comes into my vision in the future I will know I have touched it. More to the point, I have walked all of the way around it and touched it at intervals. I have also been inside it. It is quite posh, even a wedding reception was being held there, and I have got loads of photographs of it, on it, around it, even me and the Opera House in the background, another dream come true.

We decided to take a meal on the outskirts and watch the sunset and see the Opera House change from daytime to night, and the lights are spectacular. The Opera House shines out in the night air and gleams off of the water; it is a wonderful sight with the bridge in the background. We enjoyed our 'tucker' but the view backward of the city all lit up was marvellous. This really is a fine city with plenty to do and explore.

This morning we are hitting the shops. There is such a variation in ornaments but we went for the usual: a bright red T-shirt with 'Australia' printed on it, a good old diggers hat with dangling corks on threads, a fantastic plaque in the shape of the

WHAT A WAY TO TRAVEL

islands of Australia with the Sydney Opera House embossed in copper with the Harbour Bridge in the background and a rubber cut in the shape of the Opera House, a kangaroo wearing his cork hat together with little Joey showing his head out of the pouch, and another little kangaroo with a long tail and furry coat and a koala bear with his hat on and carrying the Australian flag. Outside one shop a massive koala bear sat, and we posed behind it for our photographs. Unfortunately it collapsed so we ran away quickly but returned and put it right.

For lunch we consumed local fish and chips and sat around the harbour watching everybody buzz around and stop and wonder at the Opera House and bridge. We sat looking at seagulls diving for food, the sailboats and yachts coming and going. To me this is the most beautiful harbour in the world. It is so picturesque, clean and beautiful. You can sit for hours and just watch the world go by.

We, however, are off on an adventure. A Captain Cook Cruise adventure. We will be cruising the waters around the Opera House and under the bridge, then across the water to Taronga Park Zoo. Australia has always had unique animals and reptiles only bred in these lands. On show cute little koala bears sitting in their trees. You can view them from a higher level. They are so sort of slow-moving, sort of sleepy and clinging. Then there are the crocodiles, alligators, monkey compound, elephants, giraffes, camels, and kangaroos, emus, bears, tigers but the best has got to be the kangaroos. The Big Reds take just a couple of leaps and seem to jump from one end of their compound to the other. There were mums with their young crawling in and out of pouches. Some went in headfirst and just disappeared.

And there are great sign posts like Down Under Tracks and Australian Walkabout. We had our Aussie T-shirts on and dangling cork hats and posed under them for photographs. Our last visit was to the aquarium; it was amazingly laid out with good lighting but also speakers giving sounds from the deep. You can see sharks, seals and platypus. It was a really interesting visit; the animals with their movements and habits made it good fun. After some better 'tucker' and a few tinnies of Aussie lager we spent the evening around the Kings Cross area. It is a bit of a red-light district but if you ignore that side of it, there is plenty going on down there and good restaurants.

We got up with the lark today because we intend on having a lark. We are off to the beach, not just any old beach but none other than Bondi Beach. Even the name sounds fab and it is. To get there we used a local train but got the surprise of our lives when the train pulled in. It was like a double decker bus. It had upstairs and downstairs, stacks of space inside and you could choose which way you wished to face, as the seats were reversible.

Once we reached Bondi Beach we walked down an incline across open green grass. A small shopping area, which adds to its splendour, all secluded within an arched bay. It is probably about half a mile long and a few hundred yards in depth and covered by white soft sand and a clean deep blue sea, which rolls in vigorously. It is ideal for board surfing, hand sailing and sailing. As luck would have it on our day there competitions were taking place between rival coastguards which included racing into the sea, swimming and rowing the boats, each member taking part. It was fascinating to watch very competitive and great entertainment for the day. One thing I noticed, the sun rose from the right and set on the left – or was it just the way I was facing?

Our last night in Australia we spent in different bars mixing with the Aussies and joining in their local pastime, drinking. We enjoyed their company and humour. On the way back through the park we literally stumbled across the Statue of James Cook and saw a possum up a tree. The trees in the park were beautifully decorated with tiny white lights throughout the branches. Back at the hotel room with my head in the sink I noticed the water did go anti-clockwise down the plughole.

As we left Sydney we had to make a detour to Melbourne. I have had to mention this, as I am a 'Neighbours' follower.

But I plan on returning to Australia. There is so much more I wish to see, such as Ayers Rock, go into the outback, mix with the Aborigines and, of course, visit the Great Barrier Reef. We will probably take an around the world flight ticket and stopover in the Philippines and Fiji, perhaps a few other places.

THAILAND – BANGKOK - PATTAYA

Flight delayed today by ten hours before we touched down at Bangkok airport and the first thing that hit us was the humidity and temperature. It was over 120°F today and it felt so hot I even sweated up just by standing still. We booked into our hotel. It was like a white palace on the river with a doorman and red carpet over the steps leading to the reception. It had four restaurants, a massive outdoor swimming pool and many other amenities, but above all it had the Thai people, and what a welcome they gave us. The ladies were dressed in long colourful silk gowns with their long, thick jet-black hair tied back. Their palms of the hands were together as though in prayer and against their chest and with gently bowing their heads and slight dip of their hands they said the word, 'Sawasdee' which is a welcome greeting and a smile which is so infectious you cannot help but smile back. But then Thailand is known as the land of smiles. We hurriedly checked in and dumped our cases down. What with the ten hours we had lost we wanted to get out there with the people as soon as possible. Out there on the streets is just incredible. The main street is packed with people – even at this late hour people are still shopping for vegetables and groceries. There are all sorts of cooking going on which adds incredible smells and flavours to the midnight air. The traffic is chock-a-block, bumper to bumper. Mopeds go buzzing by, horns blasting and tuk-tuks are in abundance. Added to this the humidity, the heat, the dust, the noise, the smells of cooking, the rubbish, the stagnant water and sewage and the river, plus the noise of bartering for bargains in a foreign language, gave the entire place a unique atmosphere and it is brilliant to be part of it.

We bought tiny mirrored decorated elephants, brightly gold-coloured elephants, T-shirts which are exact replicas of famous names but at 10% of the cost, a gold Buddha statue in a case and my prize possession, two Thai classic dolls of a man and woman in full traditional costume holding hands together with a silver full dress and golden tiered head dress ending in a point, and gold accessories, belt and necklace. Not to mention enough socks with the famous logos to last a lifetime. So this was our first night in Bangkok and we just knew we were going to love it here. It had everything; excitement, activity, variation and a particular buzz about the place.

Our first trip this morning is to the Grand Palace and this really is a Grand Palace. As soon as I entered the grounds my mind cast back to the film and television series of *The King and I* starring Yule Brynner as the King of Siam. I remember all the finely decorated rooms, the children, the authority the King had and that everybody had to be lower than the King, and the wonderful scene where the English school teacher and the King did a marvellous dance scene, and I am actually here to see it and touch it for myself.

The palace itself is a procession of small, triangular round domes. The outside ones are coloured white. Then you have the palace buildings and at a higher level the Golden Dome. This is quite magnificent. It is so splendid and stands out like the central structure and the height and width is unbelievable, especially when you consider that at regular periods it is again gold-plated with gold leaf But it is spectacular just how it shines out at you. As you go through the main gates the two huge warrior statues, holding a type of weapon and wearing a mystical mask with staring eyes, confront you. It is a symbol of immense power and colourfully decorated. Surrounding this area are small temples with incense joss sticks and candles smouldering. As you enter the palace buildings they are still well-preserved with markings and gold-trimmed antiques. In one of the temples is the Emerald

WHAT A WAY TO TRAVEL

Green Buddha. We had to leave our shoes outside as we entered the temple. It was dark inside but also had its own singular odour. But there, high above the altar, is the Golden Buddha. The green emerald face makes your viewing magnified and it is so awe inspiring sitting there with his legs crossed. As we left the building I put my arm around my brother Steve and sang the words, 'He ain't heavy, he's my Buddha.' Steve was grinning from ear to ear. As you go to the higher level you come to the base of the Golden Dome and supporting the lower ledge is a procession of tiny masked figurines. Their stature is that, say, of weight lifting, except their palms are up top and pointing away from each other. The legs take on the same shape but opposite way round. They look splendid as though they are supporting the full weight and their costumes are mirrored in decoration and coloured glass. A super photograph is to sit between two of them with the marble base and gold structure at the background. The whole grounds are covered in ornaments and gold structures and the decoration and colours are quite exquisite.

But oh boy, it is hot here. I am dripping with sweat; my hair is so wet it looks like I have only just washed it. It is soaking. It was great to get on the coach for a while and feel the air conditioning. Our next stop was to a gem factory. Although the jewellery was beautiful to look at I felt more interested in getting a drink down me. I needed the moisture. But our next stop was to cool us down completely. A motor-powered boat ride through a river system. The whole area was covered in thick grassland but in between were the stilted shacks of the local inhabitants, the river people. The motor boat zoomed along at tremendous speed, sending ripples to the bank and sending a fine water spray onto us. It felt quite refreshing but as we turned into a clearing we were amazed to see a gigantic floating market with a thatched bamboo roof and hundreds of small rowing boats, usually with one or two occupants, floating and drifting in every direction. Their cargo, everything and anything you could imagine. Some were actually cooking on board, others supplying vegetables, fruits while others worked in tandem supplying their wares. Others cooked and some ferried the end product to the customer.

It was a beehive of activity, with everybody bustling for space yet at the same time a kind of unwritten rule and understanding between each other. Everybody seemed to get their opportunity to sell their wares; extremely fascinating to watch.

We got off onto the main platform, which held an open stalled market with local arts and crafts, clothing and souvenirs for sale. We discovered a four-foot high wooden carving of an elephant with huge white tusks posed for a photograph. But posing more than me was a banana girl; her mother had dressed her in a pretty red and white dress. Her hair was up and a tiara placed on top. The young girl was so cute and pretty. You can imagine most of the tourists wanted to photograph her. Now this is where her mum was clever. You could snap away as much as you liked providing you purchased a bunch of bananas first. They had cornered the market as the saying goes, 'Anybody want a banana?'

Back at the hotel we took a long, cool swim but lying in this heat every 30 seconds your whole body is wet from sweat. Even

WHAT A WAY TO TRAVEL

Steve who never usually perspires, was dripping. It was a case of continually getting back into the pool.

Mealtimes were superb. In the hotel the service is first class. I even say the best I had ever seen with their soft-spoken English, courteous manners, gleaming smiles, gentleness and warmth. It was such a pleasure talking to them and they loved to laugh.

And we made them laugh. For example, in one of the empty banqueting rooms was a plastic gold imitation Buddha with his smiling face, protruding belly and his arms raised straight into the air. Steve and I decided it would make a great photograph to stand behind him and make it look as though we were tickling him under the arms. First Steve and then myself. Unknown to us the waitresses were pointing and laughing at us. It was only on the way out that we realised it was us that were entertaining them. In the reception area two young women were giving away flowers. They were so naturally attractive and wore no make-up. To look into their eyes made you just melt away but it was time to go exploring alone. We hailed a local tuk-tuk (a taxi with three wheels, two seats in the back, a hood cover with like a motorcycle-type handlebars for steering, all painted in different colours and stickers on, together with exaggerated headlamps). It turns on a sixpence, sounds like a putting moped, zooms along and does not stop for anything. Oh, and one of our senior ladies in the group took one today. She said it had no suspension. It was as bumpy as hell, shook you all over the place and gave you a sore bum. Apart from that she declared that she had loved it. At a crossroads when he went over a bump in the road she flew off of her seat, landed on the floor and her hat flew out the

WHAT A WAY TO TRAVEL

back, never ever to be seen again. It sounds just like the sort of thing that we would love. We jumped in and shouted 'Patpong'. This is the red-light district of Bangkok. We go to these types of places just to observe and soak up the atmosphere on the streets. It is always thriving with people and usually accompanied by some sort of night market, which are always fascinating to stroll around. OK OK. We did buy one naughty book but only out of curiosity and a present for a mate back home who lives alone! Back at the hotel our room was on the top floor and we had a marvellous view of the Chao Phya river at night with tiny white lights fading into the darkness and the landing stages and hotels all lit up.

Breakfast is a vast array of dishes to choose from and the standard of cooking is excellent. We are off on a tour today deep into the countryside, which will give us a good feeling of the land and people outside of the cities. Our destination is the Thai village cultural show at the Rose Garden.

Driving out of the city the local surroundings change dramatically. The roadside shops and food halls take on a whole different dimension. These would be visited more by farmers and peasants rather than by tourists. The dust and dirt is evident. We stopped along the way at a coconut grove; drinking in the juice and eating the contents was a mistake. The rest of the day I kept discovering pieces of coconut which had become stuck in my teeth, but it was delicious. The landscape turned very agricultural with fields of rice and grain. We also stopped at a salt farm, which is manufactured over here in the fields. I actually tasted it. It was definitely salt but like no other I had tasted before.

As soon as we arrived at the Thai village it was lunchtime. Great long tables of food were spread out before us. It was a pick your own choice system. We were quickly ushered into the main arena, as the floorshow was about to begin. First on the traditional Thai women dancers with the particular music sounds and the flowing brightly coloured tunics and the movements of the dancers made it a great start. Next were the men dancing sword fighting. Sparks flew off of the swords as the men struck blows but were blocked by their opponent. They spun on the spot, leaped into the air, jumped over a swinging sword, all done at a very high speed with the men letting their aggression out by yelling. Next up was cockfighting. The men baited the cocks to fight. No real harm was done to either cockerel; it was just an exhibition of one of their sports. The ladies brought on long bamboo sticks. The men joined and started to dance, hop and skip over the bamboo. The men were at full speed as the bamboo clapped together. As it opened like a flash of lighting the man would step in between, then skip high as the bamboo slammed together again. You had to be very fit, quick and nimble to dance like that and have precision timing. A boxing ring was erected in front of us. Two Thai kick boxers entered the ring with the referee. The music started to play and the boxers went through their warm-up ritual. The bell sounded for the first round and it was all action. Punching, kicking and kneeing each other. For three rounds they went at each other doing high kicks to each other's head until one finally delivered the knockout punch.

The final act was the farewell dance. A parade was led with dancing and singing, which was extremely colourful. Then a decorated elephant entered the arena draped with red silk and headpiece. It had huge white tusks, which stood out. On its back it carried a canopy with a man and woman riding inside. A huge cheer went up at the end, as this was a splendid show of skill and local cultures, a highly recommended visit.

Outside the arena were the beautiful gardens with many varieties of flowers. Around the outskirts, local arts and crafts were being shown. The silk worm spinning its thread and showing how this is manufactured into silk, paintings of local scenes, umbrella making and the painting of the decorative outside.

One section was for the elephant rides. I had always wanted to ride an elephant but as you climb the steps to a higher level to get on you realise just how wide they really are. I nearly split myself in two just trying to get astride its huge body frame. And then it just nonchalantly strolls away, wobbling its huge frame, whereas you actually experience at least a four-foot swing from side to side. As you look down you see just how high up you are. The elephants then treated us to their showpiece – hauling large tree trunks with their tusks out of the water with sheer ease. The power and delicacy of these animals is immense. The ringmaster asked for some *50* men from the audience, volunteers to have a tug of war against an elephant. Steve and I jumped at the chance. Holding onto the rope attached around the elephant we posed for our photographs. Then the order was given to take the strain. All the men got into their pulling positions. 'Heave,' was shouted. We pulled for all our might. It seemed to be working very slowly. The elephant was moving backwards but then the young lad on top of the elephant gave a slight dig in with his heels and the elephant effortlessly moved forward. We, however, shot forward about six feet. It was no contest. They were just playing with us and we stood no chance. But there again, how many people do you know who has had a tug of war against an elephant and lived to tell the tale?

It was a superb visit and a highly entertaining day. On the road back to Bangkok we passed local farmers with their horse-drawn carts loaded with the day's toll of fruit, vegetables, hay and straw, heading for the large markets of Bangkok.

Our last evening in Bangkok. We decided to take a leisurely boat ride down the river. We were amazed to see so many fish jumping out of the water. They say the water is so hot that they jump into the air just to cool down and take in some oxygen. Along the banks small children were playing and diving into the water. Once we reached our destination we would walk back to the hotel and sample the atmosphere on the streets of Bangkok for the last time. And it is still so fascinating. Although an incident did happen between two local street gangs from opposite cafés. A fight broke out in front of us, and then they smashed in each other's cafés. Then we heard a shot being fired, a policeman stood there with his gun pointing at them. He ordered them to lay down in the street with their hands behind them. We left then, but all of this going on around you just adds to your emotions and memories, but it is time to pack again and move on. Some of the girls in our group have now added two extra cases each because of the extra clothes they have purchased.

WHAT A WAY TO TRAVEL

PATTAYA

This is a beach resort. Our hotel is only 100 yards from the sand and sea but it also has a fantastic swimming pool with a central bar. Palm trees surround the pool area. We have a couple of days here to relax from our heavy schedule and to top up our tans. Got up this morning, put on our swimming trunks and got ready for a day sunbathing. Wrong. It was raining but not like rain at home. This was a monsoon. The winds were blowing sun umbrellas over and everywhere was flooded. Being Brits we still hit the beach. The rain and sea were both warm. It was still fun swimming in the Gulf of Siam and it did not take long for everywhere to dry up after the rain had ceased. Huge giant ants ran around and as it dried, swarms of mosquitoes invaded the air and we were mobbed, splatting them as we ran towards the hotel. I now know how King Kong felt, swatting the planes on top of the Empire State Building. We enjoyed the afternoon, swimming and sunbathing, and took our evening meal on the veranda overlooking the beach and sea. As we sat eating our Chinese meal we watched the sun set over the bay. It was a beautiful setting and meal. We then took the local truck taxi to the city centre. Boy, this certainly was a boneshaker and they go so fast. Hold on!

The city centre has an electric atmosphere. There are topless bars, striptease shows and nude shows. The girls on the street literally grab you and try to get you to go into their particular bar. At one time we were frogmarched into one club. There was no entrance fee but you had to buy a beer, which was reasonably priced. It was very dark inside and we sat on a stool right up against the stage. What happened next at the show I can only hint at. Balloons were popped by darts, live eels and birds disappeared, razor blades appeared, candles blown out and bottles opened. We finished our beers and discreetly left. Wow, you will not see many shows like that. The streets are packed and many locals mixed with visitors. We met many American marines, Japanese, Aussie, French and Swedes. It was a real mixed bag. Many guys were here for three months. They had rented rooms and were sharing them with local Thai girls. Some of the men were much older than the girls. Steve and I went to a doughnut shop, bought two each and sat down to eat them. Steve was shaking my arm, saying, 'Look'. At the counter a woman was bending over and showing everything. When she sat down it was plain to see that this was no ordinary woman but a transvestite. And she had two friends. We ate up quickly and left. Outside, even at midnight it is still warm enough just to wear a vest and shorts. We finished the evening off with a beer watching the Thai kickboxing, but this was the real thing unlike the exhibition. These guys really went at each other. Guest fighters were welcome to try their luck. We saw huge French and American men get cut down to size by the tiny Thai boxers. Usually they weakened the men's legs first but it was very exciting to watch and the crowd gets very involved. Well, we have been right around the world. We have done and seen so many things and enjoyed every moment. Our next stop should have been Delhi airport in India but unfortunately the runway was closed as an aeroplane had caught fire on landing, so instead of Delhi we arrived back in London. But Steve and I have a saying when travelling, never force anything, if it is not meant to be this time perhaps you are meant to do it another time. We received £200 compensation from the travel company and put it towards our next flight. Where to? India, of course. But this time as independent travellers, not as an organised group.

INDIA - JAPAN - INDIA

DELHI - AGRA - DELHI - TOKYO - HIROSHIMA - KYOTO - TOKYO - DELHI - LONDON

After our first setback of trying to reach India we are finally on our way. The flight path takes us over Bulgaria, Iran, Afghanistan, Pakistan and finally entering India to land at Delhi airport.

This place just knocks your socks off. To me, nowhere in the world is like India. It is totally amazing. Let me start by saying that we arrived to meet temperatures of 40°C and it is so humid you fight to get a breath of cool air.

We caught the local bus from the airport to the train station. When you are sitting there on this hard piece of wood you notice the thick, black dust all around you. On the seats, floor and windows. You listen to people's conversation in a foreign tongue; you observe what they are wearing. Some men with white silk turbans, full beards, older men with wrinkled faces weathered by the sun. Women in beautiful saris of all colours, and long, thick black hair. You could smell spices, herbs, and garlic all in the air, probably from a meal eaten that day. It is just an amazing experience being here. The sights, the sounds, the masses of people, the air of excitement, thousands of people in your eyesight at any one time. A kaleidoscope of colour, a siren of noise and a multitude of faces.

WHAT A WAY TO TRAVEL

Arriving at the train station we are mobbed. Everybody wants to help us, carry bags, 'Where are you going?' 'Do you need hotel?' and 'You want taxi?' What we actually needed was a train timetable to get us to Agra. Finding it difficult to seek the information we required, and being as Steve and I were brothers, we chose two brothers to answer our questions. The train to Agra did not go until tomorrow morning at 7 am. They suggested that they took us to a hotel, then brought us back in the morning to catch the train. We said, 'OK' and put our trust and faith into them. We climbed into the three wheeled taxi and zoomed off through the streets of Delhi. It was organised mayhem out there, people diving in front of you, alongside and behind, bicycles, buses, cars and taxis like ours.

What with the constant beeping of horns, the fumes, the heat and humidity and the shouting at each other, it really was a fascinating trip being on the street level. But to experience this frenzy and buzz is a unique feeling. Our hotel was of a medium standard, clean and tidy. The brothers suggested a city tour to Old and New Delhi. We jumped at the opportunity. Zooming around in our open taxi we entered the buzz of the city. Our tour took in many old historical sights such as the Gate of India, Mahatma Gandhi statue, old temples including the Qutab Minar, which is the highest stone tower in India, and the Birla Temple, one of the most amazing stone building structures I have ever seen. It is like a Jaffa orange when opened, with its separate segments and centre. It is based on a flower design. We skirted around the very old fort and finally visited the zoo. Seeing our first white rhino and tiger but, what with travelling all day, the heat, humidity, dirt and dust, we were happy to get to bed, plus we were to rise at 5:00 a.m.

Woken up at 4:30 a.m. with a hot, sweet cup of Indian tea. We are off on a five-hour journey and are loaded into an old-style bus, which is filthy inside and out. Actually, so are we. We have not bathed or showered since we arrived in India and here the grime just seems to get attracted to you. Even our clothes are getting pretty grubby. Water does not seem to be in abundance here and is sparingly used, too. But what a thrill it was to watch Delhi waking up and coming alive. Movement, sound and another day's crust to be earned. I get the impression that here if one-man gets a job, four others just help him. There are so many people milling around, one does wonder how many jobs are actually available. But one job done very well was that of the brothers. They helped us to survive Delhi. Their information was good and well delivered. You could say they guided us, advised us and protected us. Although we did pay them well for their services and a hefty tip. They still wanted our T-shirts. I had to part with my 'Escaped from Alcatraz' T-shirt so, if you see a young man in Delhi with a black and white T-shirt with those words on it, it was him! Their last function was to book this trip. After a few hours of travelling we stopped for drinks. Passing us on the road above, camels pulled large sacks of rice. The women alongside either carried children or bundles and pots on their heads. Because the road was higher than where we were standing it made for a super photograph as we stood in front and the camels, women and children passed overhead. On the bus hardly anybody could speak English except the one gentleman in front of us. So when the bus halted for stops he would indicate how long we would stay at the particular stop. Without them we would not have had any idea. He had brightly dyed hair, which is unusual for Indians, but he will come up later in my story.

Our first visit was the Red Fort at Agra, a magnificent structure. It has red sand, brick walls in a defence line. The architecture inside is splendid and, although not being preserved in any shape or form, has survived the centuries and conditions. The floor, ceilings and walls are superbly decorated with flower shapes and temple domes. Just outside the main building was the Speaking Forum, two lines of pillars and archways with domed ceilings set at regular intervals. The acoustics were quite phenomenal. It was said the speaker could talk in a quiet whisper and in the corners some one hundred yards away you would have no problem hearing them. To demonstrate this, a young boy was sent into the middle of the courtyard, a match was lit and the young boy indicated when he heard it. Just at that moment somebody let wind and the whole group fell about laughing. But the young lad did not indicate that he had heard it. I really must control myself in company.

From the top of the fort we had our very first sight of the Taj Mahal. It was way in the distance and only appeared as a small white blob on an extreme barren landscape. There seemed to be nothing around it, a few pieces of grassland, sandy soil with scattered waterbeds. But when you get there this landscape makes it even more spectacular because in this barren wilderness with nothing catching to the eye stands this brilliant white palace with its magnificent spires and white dome and, as a backdrop, nothing. It is like a mirage of sheer beauty standing out on an open, flat plain. It is breathtaking, beautiful and we cannot wait to get there, it is our next stop.

After negotiating the souvenir sellers and beggars you reach the outskirts after a few wooden structures and, your eyes adjusting to the darkness, all of a sudden you enter through the last doorway. As your eyes adjust to the bright sunlight and focus, there it stands in all its magnificence and splendour – the Taj Mahal. It is totally breathtaking. Steve and I were speechless for a few seconds just trying to take in where we were and this superb structure in front of us. You can approach either to the left or the right, which is separated by a water trough and lined with groomed shrub trees. The pathway is some 100 yards to walk. The excitement builds as the Taj Mahal grows in size and stature. There is a mid-point section which is raised up. Standing on the square makes for a brilliant photograph with the Taj Mahal as a backdrop. But the view never stops surprising you. Your first impression could be that it is small, but the reason for that is there is nothing for you to compare it against. Yet as you approach it, the building zooms to an incredible size. It is a bit like an illusion. It will change with different angles. The main building is built on a platform some 20 feet high. Everything is either white brick or white marbled facing. There are four pillars, one in each corner. The centre structure is square with picturesque archways cut into it. On top are two small domes and the centre top is a massive dome finished by a golden spire with three bulbs. At this point we wanted to touch it and feel it

WHAT A WAY TO TRAVEL

with our hands, letting its history and significance flow through our fingertips. We walked completely around the structure touching, feeling and photographing. A brilliant photograph is standing in the huge archway with arms outstretched showing the size, magnitude and finely decorated walls. Before you enter inside you are requested to either remove your shoes or cover them with a type of canvas sock complete with tie-ups. So many people had misplaced shoes it was worth a few rupees for the sock. Also they made for a great photograph. Once inside it is very dark but peaceful, with guides talking only in whispers and telling their tales and stories of years gone by and the gift of the Taj Mahal to a Princess. Time was getting on for us, as we had to get back for the bus. But as we strolled down the pathway opposite side to that we had walked up we took our last glances at such a magnificent building, and reminded each other that our dad had stood here somewhere before us during the Second World War, and now we were walking in his footsteps and seeing the exact same sight. One last glimpse to lock into our memory bank then it was gone from view. We wanted one more thing. A little white chalk replica of the Taj Mahal. Steve and I found a young enthusiastic Indian boy who carefully wrapped them in wooden cases to protect them from our still very long journey ahead. One last thing to say if you get the opportunity to go to India, make sure that you visit the Taj Mahal.

Our next stop was a silk warehouse. Rolls and rolls of silk and every colour under the sun. The brightest reds, yellows and greens, light and dark shades in each colour. Some were patterned or had gold designs throughout the length. This was a very popular stop for most of the travellers on the bus. This was the material used to make the women's saris. We, however, discovered a room in the basement. It held the most wonderful assortment of replicas of the Taj Mahal. There were marble ones, decorated ones, even ones sitting on light bulbs which would glow in the dark. It was fascinating seeing the local craftsmanship. Steve was so tempted but getting it home safely presented another problem.

We stopped and visited many temples on the return trip. One that stands out was the Hari Krishna centre. As we were the only English-speaking on board we had our own guide. Once inside the temple after removing our shoes, an incredible aroma hit us, burning incense and sticks. Flowers were placed over our necks and the singing and chanting began. We were invited to sign a special book or have a brick with our name on it for a fee. People from all over the world had left their name and country. We declined and slipped away back into the darkness outside. While waiting for the rest of the group to arrive we watched many young monks with shaved heads and the orange-coloured cloaks milling around and going about their business. As luck would have it we found an old man with crossed legs sitting on the floor, playing his magical pipe and the snake appearing and doing its mystical movements and dancing to the music. When the music stopped then the snake disappeared.

Back on the bus we were heading back to Delhi and would not arrive until one o'clock in the morning. As we had left the previous hotel at this moment in time we had nowhere to stay the night. It was rather worrying to be on the streets of a major city in the darkness of the night. As we were discussing what we would do, we pulled into a rest area for our final stop before Delhi. Since being in India we had not eaten or drunk very much and with this heat it was particularly important to keep taking in fluids. From England we had bought a bottle of orange and water and a few sandwiches. We both still had one sandwich left but by now it had sweated up and did not look too appetising but, being hungry, beggars cannot be choosers. I took one bite, yuk; it was warm and gooey. Steve said, 'Just imagine it is a breast of chicken.' We smiled and munched away with our imagination running wild – that, or we were cracking up.

I went to the toilet. Our Indian friend in front of us on the bus with ginger hair had his trousers down around his knees and was tucking himself in. As I approached him I asked, 'Are you staying in a hotel tonight?' He nodded yes, so I asked him, 'Can we stay with you at your hotel tonight?' He looked shocked. I then asked, 'How much?' Stunned, he replied, '60 rupees', and ran out still doing his trousers up. I do not think I handled that situation very well. I did not pick my words too good. I told Steve, who just fell about laughing. He reckoned the Indian thought I was chatting him up to pick him up for the night. Still, everything worked out well. When he stood up to get off of the bus he beckoned us to follow. At the hotel he did all the talking and got us booked in. It was very cheap, approximately £3 each. Our room was right up the top and it had two single beds in it, a spinning ceiling fan, a wash area which you could not use and a toilet hole in the ground with no pot, seat or toilet paper. Why should we care? By now we were black with dirt, filthy, smelly but happy as pigs in shit!

WHAT A WAY TO TRAVEL

This is India and we loved every minute of it To celebrate we went down and ordered a bottle of water each. Remember to get sealed tap water, as it has been known for people to pour local water in and sell it to tourists. But to us this was a bottle of the finest champagne. In our room we toasted each other, drank wildly, talked about our day, our experiences, feelings and wrote up our diaries. We posed for photographs, one over the open toilet with our shorts at half mast, our dirty, smiling, unshaven faces and lying on the bed with its one sheet holding our bottle of precious water. The bed was as hard as rock. I jumped up and down on it. Steve stopped me in the nick of time as I nearly jumped and put my head in the revolving fan blades. The night was hot and sticky. We went out onto the main balcony and looked down on the street below. People were sleeping everywhere, in boxes, the back of trucks, on the ground. It was literally littered with people just sleeping anywhere they could. Then a motorbike roared up the street. It must have disturbed and woken everybody. Apparently not, they did not move and just slept on, oblivious to the commotion around them. Exhausted by now we laid on our beds, keeping our clothes on. They were now welded to us. We fell into a deep sleep but only for a few hours for as soon as the sun rises then so do the people. The noise, hustle and bustle of a new day begins.

We decided to take a bike taxi back to the centre from where we would catch our bus to the airport. We found a lovely little old man and his three-wheeled bike that spoke good English. He told us many stories on our journey, taking us through the busy shopping streets, seeing, and being part of the street life.

WHAT A WAY TO TRAVEL

At one time we got entangled with another bike travelling in the opposite direction. After a few choice words, shouting and hollering we were on our way. He dropped us at the main terminal. This really was the centre, like a circular roundabout with shops in the middle and eight lanes of traffic to contend with. We just stood and watched for an hour, the traffic on the streets and the people on the pavements. It was sheer entertainment looking at the clothing, fashions, the faces, what they carried or even what they were eating. The bus got us back to the airport. First duty was the washroom. We tipped the attendant first, that gave us a good service, clean towels, soap, stripped to our waists and washed vigorously; cleaning my teeth for the first time in days was heaven sent, and spraying my armpits was total bliss. Mind you, we did get some strange looks from those entering the washroom. Once the water flowed away in the sink the tide mark left was black, but at last my hair itched no more. Second stop was the restaurant. We ordered two meals each. Two bottles of coke each and four cups of tea each. We pigged out and drank as much as possible then had a little snooze. Checked in, boarded the plane, took a few beers, food was served – rice with chicken curry – hit a bit of turbulence and Steve brought the whole lot back up into a paper bag. While Steve slept it off, I struck up a conversation with an English guy who lived in India. We swapped stories and time flew by. Excuse the pun. Before we knew it, we were descending to land at Tokyo airport, Japan, land of the Rising Sun, ready for our next adventure. We got off of the plane.

JAPAN
UENO – TOKYO – HIROSHIMA - TOKYO

The flight took us over Bangladesh and Burma. Before landing at the most automated country in the world everything seemed so clean, pristine and organised. Also everybody is dressed clean and tidy. Businessmen and women in suits, children in uniforms.

Now imagine the culture shock for us. We had just arrived from a third world country and now entered the land containing some of the richest men in the world. We actually thought that we might not be allowed entry at passport control. We arrived looking none the better for wear, unshaved, scruffy and dirty around the edges. Our welcome was none too friendly as the whole contents of our rucksacks were displayed out in front of us. Even our Taj Mahals in their little wooden boxes were vigorously shaken. The soles on Steve's joggers were ripped back, possibly looking for drugs as we had flown in from India. But once through this spectacular modern airport you had access to trains, metros, limousines and taxis to take you to your next destination. We saw advertising signs for Tokyo's Disneyland but our plan was to take a local train to a suburb of Tokyo, as it would be less expensive as the city and a good base to travel to and from. We selected a place called Ueno.

Travelling on the train was fascinating watching people coming and going and, although we did not mean to stare, it was incredible observing their faces and mannerisms. Although they looked back at us they never seemed to stare but would just glance in our direction. If our eyes were to meet they

WHAT A WAY TO TRAVEL

would look away quickly but we also noticed so many would close their eyes resting, relaxing or snoozing. Getting off at Ueno was well planned. We fell in love with the place. It was sheer fun and interesting communicating with them. We saw a tram advertising board with Japanese writing on and we took photographs standing next to it. Also a poster board with a beautiful Japanese woman on it. We pretended to be kissing her to take a photograph. Some young girls opposite were laughing hysterically.

We climbed the steps of the station, which led us to the streets outside. The city centre was a magnitude of office towers, banks and companies. There were glass buildings everywhere. The pavements and roads were spotless. There was no litter or rubbish whatsoever. The streets were lined with all kinds of restaurants, shops and an inside and outside market. On one of the buildings was a plastic model of King Kong climbing the building and leaving white footprints behind him. Our first task was to book into a hotel. We found one that looked pleasant from the outside. The entrance was strange, across paving stones in shingle. A Geisha lady welcomed us by bowing. We bowed back and asked, 'Are there any rooms available?' 'Yes,' she replied and we asked, 'How much?'

The price given was quite reasonable, we started to complete the booking forms and then asked was breakfast included. She replied, ''No, only here for four hours.' We said, 'Four hours! We sleep the night.' 'No,' she answered, 'This is a love hotel, where you book a room just for the afternoon.' We got out of there as fast as we could.

WHAT A WAY TO TRAVEL

Our next call was a great deal simpler. A four-star hotel. Considering where we had been sleeping the last few nights it was time to pamper ourselves. It was a beautiful hotel and the room was spectacular. Laid out for us in our room, a comb, toothpaste, shampoo, hair gel and aftershave.

Steve and I took our first baths in days. After washing and shaving we put on our kimonos and slippers that had been left in the room. Standing there we could not resist a photo shoot. Posing in a karate stance and bowing with our hands clasped together made for brilliant photographs. Also in the room, tea-making facilities but with a difference. Green coloured tea, no milk or sugar but quite tasty all the same. Clean and smart, we headed for the local McDonalds and filled our stomachs, but it was another great place to observe the Japanese way of life. The place was full of children all in school uniforms. Everybody was chatting and laughing away. It was lovely just listening to the language being spoken and the laughter. They certainly seem to be a happy band of people with a good sense of humour. Looking out through the glass windows we watched people go about their business. Young five-year-old children walked to school alone and crossed main roads. Crime rate is extremely low where people can walk the streets and feel safe. The businessmen seem to work long hours but before they go home they either have a drink or take a meal. Some even stay over and get up early and to work. The women seem to spend their lunchtimes shopping. They are all carrying little shopping bags with something in. After yet another coffee we decided to hit the shops and markets. It was fascinating looking at their food stocks, all kinds of rice and vegetables, dried fish, and live fish, noodles etc. The shops are very colourful, filled with Japanese products, watches, televisions, compact discs, radios, pocket televisions and all of the latest mod cons. We also came across buildings filled with ball bearing machines. The Japanese play these machines for hours and hours. You exchange your money for a box of ball bearings then you feed them in. They zoom through the machine at high speed and if you are lucky they fall into certain holes, and if they do you win more balls. Some people had crates full of balls, which they either exchange for gifts or money. Steve and I exchanged a few Yen and had a go. It was over in seconds; some came back out, which I put back in. Actually there were more balls on the floor than what I had actually won. But sitting there we took a photograph, putting our little metal balls in. The noise of the place, metal smashing about everywhere, then when somebody hits a jackpot lights flashed and sirens sounded. It was fascinating to see but mind-boggling to understand.

Back on the streets we took photographs of us both standing in the street with all the neon signs above us and flags dangling with Japanese writing on. Also the people. We seemed to look so tall in the street. We also went to enquire about these hotels which had glass capsules instead of beds to sleep in. We got in the lift and went two floors, the doors opened and we walked out, only to be met by the receptionist screaming at us, shouting and hollering. We dived back into the lift; a man came in and asked if he could help us. We explained exactly what we wanted to do and he informed us why we were shouted at. It was because we had kept our shoes on and shoes were not allowed to be worn inside. There were no signs but we had seen enough and left. We decided to eat a traditional Japanese meal. It was fun choosing one and going into different restaurants and bars. Everybody seems very happy, laughing and drinking. The men and women mixing well. We decided on one which showed pictures outside on the menu, we needed to, although English was widely spoken and understood. It was still difficult to communicate what you wanted at times, so we pointed to our bowl of soup. Well, not actually a bowl, more like a bucket was served up. I think it was called everything soup because it certainly had everything in it. Noodles, seaweed and lots of other ingredients – I know not what they were. But it was very tasty and filling. We strolled around the streets looking at the very many bars, Karaoke bars, massage parlours and watched the suited businessmen stumble around drunk. Probably from too much sake. They might work hard but they certainly party hard as well. We had a late night coffee at Mac's and thought about where we were and what a super day it had been, and started to make plans for the rest of our stay here. Then it was back to our super beds and dreamland. Oh! It was so soft and cosy.

Well, today we got up, packed our clothes and headed for the capital of Japan. Tokyo. This was to be totally different to Ueno. Bigger, noisier, more people, traffic jams, traffic fumes, larger streets and buildings too, huge hotels of a very high class. And we still enjoyed ourselves bustling along with the crowds. We visited the Meiji Shrine set in extensive naturally wooded grounds. This most popular and impressive shrine is

WHAT A WAY TO TRAVEL

dedicated to Emperor Meiji, who is often called the 'Father of Modern Japan'. Entrance is through a large wooden structure. It is very peaceful here with over 100,000 shrubs and trees within the grounds. A code of etiquette is to be observed when praying in a shrine. You must be appropriately dressed for the occasion, pass under the Torii and walk through the Sando, go to the handwashing stone basin and cleanse your hands, with a dipper pour water into your cupped hand then bring the water to your mouth and gargle. Advance before the god enshrined, then throw some money into the offertory box. Then bow deeply twice. After that clap your hands twice. Then make a deep bow once more. We were fortunate to watch a wedding ceremony while we were there. The bride looked fantastic in her traditional Japanese outfit. We, of course, took photographs of the couple.

The possibility of there being a lack of something to do is definitely remote in Tokyo. Look at the choices, movies, theatres, imported and domestic, family entertainment at many amusement parks, Disneyland, baseball stadium, zoological park, concerts and recitals, rock and jazz sessions, theatres, halls and clubs. There are seven resident symphony orchestras, operas, ballets, Kabuki theatres, bars, pubs, piano bars, Karaoke singing bars, beer halls, discos, Geisha shows or a Sumo wrestling bout. You may even catch exhibition bouts in Judo, Kendo, Karate, Kyudo and Aikido or you could just stroll the streets taking in the atmosphere, look at the colourful neon signs and the brightly lit Tokyo tower.

After staying the night in Tokyo in the morning we got up and headed for Tokyo train station. Standing under the Tokyo train station sign we posed for our photo shoot. Today we are catching the Bullet train over half the length of the island of Honshu to the city of Hiroshima. Negotiating the tickets, price and platform number was not too easy but the staff was extremely patient with us. On the platforms we noticed women outnumbered the men when the trains pulled in. It was like a mass stampede, the people had to be pushed in by the porters to be able to close the doors. We, however, had reserved seats for the five and quarter hours' journey. This train in something else, spacious, clean and tidy. It pulled out of the station spot on time but the train just seemed to glide. The trip was so smooth. You could hold a glass of water without any ripples appearing on the surface. Also, a very low noise is given off. The train will reach speeds of 220 km per hour. Now I know why it is called the Bullet train. It is a great way to travel and to see so much of the country in a small space of time. Passing through industrial towns and cities we noticed famous national company names such as Canon, Minolta, Mitsubishi and many others. The countryside was very green with lots of surface water around. We saw tiny villages with little houses and carparks full of brand new cars. Then we got our first glimpse of Mount Fuji, its peak still covered in snow. It is a remarkable sight – with a flat, surrounding area it really stands out and depending on the time of day, the season and weather the view is forever changing. The journey was fast and comfortable and you are served drinks and a light meal. A young lady pushes the trolley and sings out her wares in a high pitched voice. It sounded so sweet. We imagined her singing out, biscuits, chocolates, tea, and coffee.

WHAT A WAY TO TRAVEL

The train pulled into Hiroshima station spot on time. Getting off we photographed this magnificent train and posed under the Hiroshima train sign. Our first call was to a business hotel. These are slightly lower in price but have adequate rooms and quality. After travelling for most of the day we decided to take a meal. We found a local café and sat down. A little Japanese man who was drunk sat down next to me. He ordered us beers and we were talking and laughing together until he put his hand on my leg and asked, 'Let's all go back to your hotel, I love arse.' We left that place faster than the Bullet train that brought us here.

We got up early this morning as today was going to be a full day. We took breakfast at the train station. Bacon, eggs and 2-inch thick pieces of toast plus jam and coffee. Took the local tram and, being as I could not work out how to pay or how much, I travelled free. We were heading for the Peace Memorial Park. After crossing the river, the first structure we came across was the Atomic Bomb Dome. During the Second World War, on 6th August 1945 at 8.15 am, an atomic bomb exploded over the city of Hiroshima. There right in front of us was the bomb zone, an old church. The bomb exploded in the air and the dome was directly under the epicentre. Hence why it survived when all around was total mayhem and chaos. It is a bit like the eye of the storm. The area in the eye of the storm is calm whereas outside the eye it is hurricane conditions. Just standing there looking at the shell of the building we fell totally silent. A lump filled my throat and I could feel the tears building in my eyes. We tried to imagine that day in 1945. It is impossible but the feeling of loss is overwhelming. Now we had seen the other side of war after being at Pearl Harbour and now Hiroshima. It made you realise how precious life should be and how devastating war can be.

We entered the Peace Memorial Park and observed the many monuments. There are over 59 monuments dedicated to the people who lost their lives that day and the aftermath. To me the most distressing was the A Bomb children's statue draped daily with flowers. As we passed through the park we stopped at the Memorial Cenotaph and the Flame of Peace. Feeling a bit low we were soon cheered up by the Japanese school children. The park was overrun with them. They were doing projects dressed in their school uniforms and bearing in mind this was a Saturday. We were surrounded by excitable children. Each wanted our autographs and, knowing which country we had come from, it made us feel like celebrities signing autograph after autograph. Now I know how rock stars feel. We had a sandwich and drink on the park bench and fed the many pigeons in the park. Plucking up enough courage we decided to visit the museum. We watched a film and newsreels of the whole incident including the aftermath and pictures of survivors. Over 300,000 people perished from just one bomb. The remainder of the museum had photographs of the bomb and the city before and after. Photographs of people burnt from the heat, wind and black rain and radiation. There were pieces saved from the original site. Roof tiles that had melted. A watch which had stopped at 8.15 am. Clothes off of bodies, an old piano pitted with fragmented glass, also pieces of glass, which had entered people and had not been removed for over twenty years. A metal window frame bent out of all shape, which we touched as it had come from that era. On the side walls were pictures of famous people who had visited the museum, Jimmy Carter, US President, the present Pope and Mother Theresa, and we were standing where these famous people had once stood. A scene had been erected from that day showing flames and fire of the city ablaze and models of people with their clothes ripped and skin dripping off them. It had an extreme and powerful impact. Some of the Japanese school children ran out crying or hugged each other, sobbing. There was one photograph that has burned into my memory of a human being and just a trace of the outline of the body burned into the pavement. We left the building and in the park we rang the peace bell. The entire place leaves a remarkable impression, which you hope will never ever happen again, but pray for peace in our world.

We spent the rest of the day and night looking at the new city of Hiroshima built out of the ashes of the old one. It is now a modern and go-ahead, thriving city although the wounds will take a long time to heal. We had a quiet evening with a beer. In the morning we had our delicious thick pieces of toast then took the train back towards Tokyo but getting off at Kyoto. We needed a pick-me-up and this was just the place to do it. Kyoto is a sightseer's paradise. Our first stop was an old Shogun Temple; a wooden fort surrounded by a moat filled with colourful carp fish. They were huge in size. Entering the temple you got a feel of the old ancient days, warlords and Samurai warriors. We moved on to visit the Imperial Palace, a huge park with a wooden fortress. The surrounding grounds are incredible

WHAT A WAY TO TRAVEL

lakes with picturesque bridges spanning the water and superbly kept gardens of shrubs, trees and flowers. The lakes are covered in lilies and filled with fish, some a shining light gold colour. We booked into a first-class hotel. This is something else and we were treated like VIPs. It was expensive but it was time to spoil ourselves. The city at night was packed with partygoers. This was a Bank Holiday weekend. We calculated that we had spent five times as much money in Japan as we did in India for the same time span. Never mind, look at where we have got.

In the morning we left our room and the chambermaid smiled, bowed and said, 'Up your arse.' Well, Steve and I thought she had said that. We thought that perhaps it was 'Good morning' in Japanese but happened to sound English. The lift arrived and an old Japanese man was already inside. We walked in and bowed to each other and I said, 'Up your arse.' 'Up your arse,' came straight back. We held ourselves until he got out, then we just exploded into laughter. We have really enjoyed our stay in Japan. To remind us we purchased a beautiful little Japanese doll with a silk dress carrying a parasol. Also two Samurai swords on a keyring with a red tassel. But the real bonus was when we asked the hotel if we could keep the kimonos in our room. When they replied, 'Yes, no problem' we were over the moon. We took the Bullet train back to Tokyo then headed for the airport. Outside one of the shops a mannequin doll was dressed in traditional national costume. It made for a great photograph standing next to her. A flight to Iran had been cancelled and there was some 500 Iranians sprawled everywhere trying to find a spot to sleep the night. We joined them as we were going to have to spend

WHAT A WAY TO TRAVEL

the night here as well, due to a shortage of funds. At first we got strange looks but eventually we struck up conversations. They shared their food with us. A type of flat pastry with goat's cheese. I wrapped the bread around the cheese and popped it into my mouth. The cheese was so damn hot I had to spit it out into my hand. Steve asked what it tasted like. 'Good,' I replied and encouraged him to pop it into his mouth. He did and I just sat back and watched his face and expression. He hated it. But I told him not to spit it out, as it would offend our newly acquired friends. He said with a mouthful, 'I've got to.' When I showed him mine in my hand he said, 'You sod.' It was a rough old night trying to sleep on a cold, hard floor but our humour, high spirits and stories got us through it. During the night I took a photograph of Steve sprawled out on the floor with his head on his rucksack. Just to think of where we slept last night, and now look at us. But it made breakfast on the aeroplane special. Our flight path took us over Korea, before landing us back at Delhi airport – India.

Back at Delhi airport we decided not to stay in transit, as our flight home was not for 24 hours. Instead we wanted to spend it in the airport lounge and go outside when we wished to. Trying to relay this to the authorities got very complicated. We were sent to the corner of the hall, along with this huge mountain of a man, an Indian with shoulder-length hair. He was totally legless and could hardly speak but became the focus of attention and entertainment. They gave us a load of aggravation, but it was nothing compared to what he gave them. Eventually they let him through into the airport, pushing his trolley. The trolley shot forward and he fell face first to the ground. We were eventually allowed in after a shift change. We were let out on the lower level so went straight upstairs to get back in. No way, the airport security told us we were not allowed into the airport until a couple of hours before the flight, all because of security reasons and that was hours away. He said we could go and see the airport manager who would give us a pass. After all, we did have flight tickets. We knocked on the office door and were told to wait outside. Over an hour later we were called in and made to feel so small and insignificant. Needless to say he said, 'No.' So that was it. With no Indian money and no way of exchanging the money we did have we faced the prospect of our second night in a row sleeping on a hard concrete floor. Only this time it would be outdoors. Oh well, at least it is warm and dry here. Wrong again. At about 11 o'clock at night we saw the most electrifying electric storm ever. The skies lit up with the most amazing lightning show followed by a torrential downpour. More to the point, it was a monsoon. But being outside an airport it turned out to be a fascinating experience. You meet an amazing array of people whose families are turning up to say goodbye to their loved ones. One old chap, a dad, was saying goodbye to his daughter. She was emigrating to England. He was crying and upset. We got talking to him and told him not to worry as she would be OK. He was hugging us and shaking our hands and thanking us. We even got involved with the families. Some were going off on holidays, there was kissing, hugging, crying and all the waving of goodbyes. One group of young Germans ran up a little late and placed their half-drunken beer bottles in the bin. We thought someone must be looking after us and, unaccustomed to scrimmaging in bins, I was not going to miss the opportunity of a drink. That floor was damned hard to try and sleep on. Plus, by now we were filthy dirty again. We laughed when we said, 'No food, no drink, no money and no bed.' About 5 am I had enough. I approached the main door and luckily there had been a shift change in personnel. I opened the door and showed my ticket in his face and he said, 'OK'. I beckoned to Steve to hurry before he changed his mind. Then we were inside. We hurriedly changed our money and got food and drink. Then curled up on a nice soft leather chair and snoozed. Our last action was to buy a few souvenirs, a lady doll carrying a musical instrument and a metal calendar disc, which will tell the day, month and year for many years to come. But most of all because it had 'Made in India' on it and we had made it to India and back (back home, that is) but memories to last us a lifetime.

WALES, IRELAND, EIRE, WALES, THE ISLE OF ANGLESEY

Mum, Steve and I set off in the family car. Entering South Wales we headed for the Welsh Folk Museum. There are these quaint little old houses filled with relics from the past, old clocks, radios, biscuit tins, old beds and all types of everyday objects.

Showing the items people used in days gone by, it felt like a trip down memory lane for our mum as she was born in Wales. It was like having our own personal guide. Mum explained exactly what it was like to live in those days and, of course, the war days with rationing. We think it was a treasure trove of collectors' items and thoroughly enjoyed strolling around the grounds eating home-made oven-baked cakes and rekindling the past.

Next stop was Cardiff Arms Park, home of the national Welsh football and rugby club. Although there was no match on, through the gates we could see the posts and the hallowed turf. On the floor I discovered an old ticket of the 1991 Rugby World Cup. Wales verses Australia – a souvenir for the album.

We then headed for the Rhondda Valley, birthplace of our mum. Going down and up the winding roads of valleys it reminded me of the song 'There's a welcome in the hillside'. We stopped outside the Rhondda Public House for a photo snap showing the name. Then we carried on to the row of houses, one of which mum was born in. It was a coal mining community and some of the surrounding hills used to be coal slack. Mum was amazed they were now covered in grass. Down below was the stream in which mum and her brothers played in and above the house, the old schoolhouse. Mum pointed out the exact house and we photographed it. She then went back in time and told us stories of the place names, things that had happened and we wondered if mum had never moved away would she have met our dad. Would we have existed and, what if we had been brought up here, how different would our lives have been? We asked mum if she wished to go and knock on the door of her first home. She was tempted but declined, saying that it had all changed so much now. So we moved on to Fishguard. From here we would catch a ferry to Rosslare, Ireland. We had a few hours to kill before the ferry departed so we had a pleasant meal and a pint in a local pub. We found the locals ever so warm, welcoming and friendly.

The sailing took about three and a half hours. We arrived in the early hours of the morning. It was still dark and, being as there was not much traffic on the roads, we did a few hours driving, stopping for breakfast at a farmhouse. The husband was out working the land and the wife cooked us a good, hearty Irish breakfast. It was fascinating listening to her accent and pronunciation of some words like 'three'. She was great company and we met the kids as well. That certainly set us up for the day. We headed for Waterford, as we wanted a tour around the Waterford Crystal factory.

We were first shown into the reception area to a magnificent

WHAT A WAY TO TRAVEL

display of craftsmanship of cut crystal. The display area had a full dining table filled with crystal glasses, goblets, plates, serving trays and dishes. Above hung the most incredible crystal chandelier I had ever seen. In the showcases, bowls, dishes and vases and all types of crystal trophies including a magnificent gold trophy and a world globe. A short film was shown explaining the history, training and process of crystal. Then we were taken on a guided tour of the plant. First to the materials in department, then to the furnaces where we watched men rolling, blowing and moulding the molten glass. Then to the designing, cutting and polishing. It was a totally fascinating visit and highly recommended. We were very tempted to buy but on our budget settled for the wonderful postcards.

Next stop on our tour, Cork city. Along the route we stayed in many different hotels. We always found the people to be so friendly and helpful. Generally happy-go-lucky. We pulled into a garage and put ten pounds of petrol in. I gave the man an English ten pound note and he gave me an Irish ten-pound note back. Almost the same equivalent. When I pointed out the mistake he said, 'I tort it was a twenty-pound note'. Next stop for us was Blarney Castle, home of the famous Blarney Stone. It is a lovely old castle and the tower is quite high. You ascend some narrow, steep, winding steps. Looking out of the holes in the wall you imagine firing arrows at the advancing enemy or pouring boiling oil onto them. Back to reality. The view from the top is marvellous. The Blarney Stone is on the far wall. Its location is under the main wall. There are two upright bars and lying on your back and grabbing the two bars you lower your head down through the gap. It must be a good couple of feet down and is definitely a back-breaker. When you kiss the stone it is freezing on your lips and wet. But the photographs are brilliant. You realise just how far you dip your head but my hat goes off to my mum. She managed to dip right down and kiss the stone although the guy helping to lower the people had to help pull her back up. But she did so well. The grounds of the castle are brilliant. They have fairy gardens; magnificent twisted trees, jagged stones, thick weed grass, little tunnels and wishing steps running down through the rock. Our theory was this is where the little fairies and leprechauns live. We went back to the entrance and picked up our certificate certifying that we had 'Visited the castle and had kissed the Blarney Stone and is now sent forth with the gift of Eloquence which this stone bestows', signed, 'Keeper of the castle'. I thought I was getting the gift of the gab. Mum said I had already got that. Just outside the grounds was the local post office and a lovely flat top shop called The Irish House. Mum, Steve and myself all cuddled each other and took photographs and bought some great souvenirs here. A rubber with a little, green-dressed man smoking a pipe with 'lucky' at the top and 'leprechaun' at the bottom. I kissed the Blarney Stone badge and survived. Two little pixie men with hats next to a pot of gold. An Irish lady doll dressed in traditional costume with a red headscarf. Also a brilliant collection of postcards, a man standing in the snow with no pants on showing his bottom and hitch-hiking with the words 'Bumming around in Ireland', a chap sitting in the road on a deck chair wearing only a hat, rolled up trousers and a pair of rolled down wellington

WHAT A WAY TO TRAVEL

boots reading a book with a bottle of beer, in the background a shop with O'Donoghue's on and the caption of Sunspots in Ireland. Brilliant humour. But my favourite, an old Irish home ramshackle with holes in the thatched roof and at the bottom it says, 'One more payment and it's ours'.

We went into a local café where we ordered pies and sausage rolls. Mum went first, and then myself followed by Steve. Mum and I sat down to eat our hot pies as Steve was holding his sausage roll. The young lady behind the counter said, 'Give me your sausage roll and I'll get and heat it up.' Putting it on a plate, she disappeared. Mum and I had finished our meals while Steve was still waiting for his. I suggested that I would ask for him and see what the hold-up was. Another lady said. that she would check it out. Apparently when the sausage roll was put on the plate the young lady was told a telephone call had come through for her over in the main reception area. Evidently, she crossed the courtyard with the plate in her hand and that is where they found the sausage roll, over in reception.

Eventually Steve consumed his sausage roll and we moved on, heading for Tipperary but it was a long way. Remember the song? We picked up a song sheet at the local tourist office. We booked a room in a bed and breakfast on the main street through the town. It is a lovely old Irish town with names such as Nellie O'Brien's over the pub doors. That evening we visited a few local taverns. We had a Paddy's whiskey and a few pints of the black Irish brew, Guinness to its friends. Never have I tasted one so good. When you order one it will sit for two or three minutes before it is topped up and given to you. It is thick, black

WHAT A WAY TO TRAVEL

liquid, is a brilliant blend of taste and goodness, and went down a treat. One of the pubs had a local group playing Irish songs and dancing. It all added to a unique atmosphere. The people were fantastic, friendly and chatty. Everybody seemed to be enjoying himself or herself. The next day with a bit of a thick head we headed for Limerick. We wanted to take a photograph of us all standing next to the great River Shannon. How I wished I had my fishing rod with me. We passed over this fine green land and, heading for the Curragh Horse Racing track, we came across a beautiful rainbow on the road ahead and we thought of the film *Finnigan's Rainbow* and the pot of gold at the end of the rainbow. I guess that in this case the gold is the people and the land and the fact when Irish eyes are shining, and the saying, the luck of the Irish.

Our last call was Dublin's fair city. This is where the girls are so pretty. I first met Sweet Molly Malone. It is a lovely old city full of character through its buildings and landmarks. We drove over the bridges and through the city and along the elegant O'Connell Street. We even saw an advertisement for a hotel called 'Paddy Murphy' and I just had to purchase the Pitch Black postcard. On it said 'Dublin by night' and that summed up our journey really. Fun and totally enjoyable. We also had crossed the Liffey River and would have liked to stayed longer in Dublin and soak up the atmosphere but our ferry from Dun Laoghaire to Holyhead left in just a few hours' time. We arrived back in Wales around about midnight. The local hotels stay open for late bookings so we booked straight away into a B&B and went straight to bed, feeling exhausted from our travels.

After a good breakfast we drove through the Isle of Anglesey, North Wales. The drive took us through beautiful green pastures and onto the Menai Suspension Bridge from where we got a terrific view of the Menai Straits with a wooded shoreline. The flowing river with a central island and the bridge makes for a picturesque scene. We wound our way through the hillside until we discovered that we were slightly lost. Asking a lady where we were, she replied,

'LLANFAIRPWLLGWYNGYLLGOGERYCHWYRND-
ROBWLLLLANTYSILIOGOGOGOCH'
I never asked her to repeat that but we had arrived in the longest-named town in the whole of Britain. Roughly translated it stands for 'Church Mary A Hollow White Hazel Near To The Rapid Whirlpool Church Saint Tysilio Cave Red'. Mum, Steven and I all stood outside the local post office with the full name of the place clearly marked on the outside. To take the photograph and get the whole name in you had to stand on the other side of the road. We asked the lady inside to say the name again for us. She also stamped our passport with the name. Just up the road is a quaint little old railway station with the name on the railway station sign. Standing under the sign with my arms and legs outstretched made for a superb photograph. We purchased a souvenir platform ticket from the exhibition centre across the road. Also a sticker of the Welsh flag displaying the Red Dragon and the words Cymru, the Welsh word for Wales, and another sticker saying, 'I've been to' and the name of the town and the Menai Bridge in the background. We also purchased a doll dressed in traditional clothing and a

matching badge with the costume and Wales along with Cymru on, and a postcard with the saying on, 'You may visit Bonny Scotland the lochs and glens to roam. You may spend a while in Ireland and kiss the Blarney Stone. You may wander through Old England and walk the leafy lanes. But Wales is the finest place of all except for those darned long names'. This basically summed everything up, plus mum speaking some of the Welsh language she had learnt, plus a few sayings and songs. Well, getting our bearings back we finally left the Isle of Anglesey. We headed for Caernarfon Castle, the setting for the Investiture of HRH Prince Charles as Prince of Wales. It is centuries old, a fortress and its magnificent walls have survived the period of time. Mum and I climbed the steps to one of the entrances and posed hand in hand in the doorway for our photograph with the brick wall behind us. We walked the complete perimeter of the outside of the walls. It is a brilliant setting, with the water to one side and the small shops on the other side. Leaving this area we headed for the rolling hills of Snowdonia. The scenery is spectacular, high hills and deep valleys. A little railway runs to the summit of Snowdon. The air is fresh and the walks exhilarating. The car took the strain of the high hills and the brakes heated on the descents. We left Wales and headed for home. We all agreed that we had a super trip and it was great being able to show mum what Steve and I get up to and what we get out of travelling. Being as mum gave me my start in travelling it was good to see her doing the same and going back to her roots. On the way home in the car we made plans for our next trip. Using the car we planned a trip to Scotland.

SCOTLAND

You take the high road and I'll take the low road and I'll be in Scotland before you. This was one of the many songs we sang as we drove through the night, reaching the border of Scotland in the early hours of the morning. Crossing the border we had our first photo shoot. We discovered a large erect stone with 'Scotland' painted on it. Standing under the sign with arms raised aloft it was proof we were now in Bonny Scotland, land of the brave.

Our first stop was Edinburgh and the famous castle built high on a volcanic hill. It is a magnificent landmark, steeped with history and pageantry. It fills the skyline with its splendour. From the inside we heard the magnificent sound of a Scottish piper playing the bagpipes. We crossed over the Forth Bridge and photographed the Old Forth Railway Bridge, a unique engineering feat. Travelling up and through the Scottish Highlands and the Glens, seeing the Scottish heather on the hillside, we passed through Dundalk then up to Pitlochry where there is a visitor centre and fish ladder. It was amazing just watching the salmon up-stream; the pool of water outside the dam where many fish would spring into the air and then disappear under the water. In the observation room you can watch them enter the tank and then disappear into the tube

WHAT A WAY TO TRAVEL

helping them to get further up-stream. We, however, travelled on up to the Grampian region and the Spey Valley, stopping at Aviemore, a holiday resort with every provision for both indoor and outdoor sport and recreation. It is primarily a winter sports centre and there are consequently many nearby ski slopes and lifts.

For lunch we had haggis covered in batter and chips. A take-away meal. It was not to our liking, hence the first every flying haggis. When it landed, a dog ran up, sniffed the haggis, then bolted off. It seems it was not to his liking either.

Our next stop was somewhere I had always wanted to come to. Loch Ness. Well, I have always been a believer in Nessie, the Loch Ness monster. We arrived by the waterside and I just wanted to touch the water and paddle around in it with no socks on. Mum and I set about building our own monster. We found a huge stone and some logs. Then stood next to it to be photographed.

We visited the Loch Ness Centre and watched film clippings and still photographs of Nessie. To me they looked totally realistic and we read the reports of statements from people who swear they have seen Nessiteras Rhombopteryx, or 'Nessie' for short. We purchased postcards of the artist's impression of Nessie. Also a plastic replica with its long neck and tail. Standing next to many signs we had our photographs taken. Whether it is true or not, does it really matter? It is fun to believe and, who knows, one day... We decided to take a picnic lunch by the loch. As we approached, a lone piper in full traditional Scottish dress, and that included a kilt and sporran, played beautiful piped music. It

WHAT A WAY TO TRAVEL

was a wonderful setting, the loch, green grass, the music, good food and a drink and just constantly looking at the water for perhaps that one glimpse, and of course the good company.

Steve and I tried to play a trick on mum. We tied our plastic Nessies to a branch on a tree and took a photograph. We hoped that when it would be developed it would look like Nessie swimming on the loch. But unfortunately the string was too visible, although I must admit it looks really good. After lunch we drove back through Drumnadrochit and headed for the Inverness area of the Scottish Highlands and Islands. Beautiful scenery of rolling hills. From the top we could see for miles in every direction. Tonight our bed would be in the Dunroamin Hotel. As we really had done enough roaming for one day. The evening meal was poached salmon washed down with a glass of Sheep's Dip whiskey, a local delicacy. But what a name to give it. We stayed in the hotel bar and enjoyed an evening of chat with the locals and their broad Scottish accents.

This morning's trip will take us right up to the top of the map, to John O'Groats. Well, we had all been to Land's End. But this completed it all for us now to be at the other end. The distance between the two is 876 miles, from here to London it is 690 miles. We had great fun photographing the area, standing on rocks with the sea behind you. The signpost John O'Groats, the last house and another saying, 'First and Last in Scotland' and the signpost pointing in different directions to different destinations and giving the mileage. When we were there it said 'Gone to lunch 31st May 1989'. We bought a few souvenirs, an air freshener card with a set of bagpipes on and saying, 'Breath of the Highlands' and a little wee Jimmy man with his tartan hat on. We pinned badges to him, one of the thistle and Scotland. The second a piper and John O'Groats plus a super postcard showing the sea and the rock face of land and two figures standing on the rock, saying, 'Us'. We made it to John O'Groats and at the bottom 'Where Scotland Ends'. Duncansby Head John O'Groats. Travelling back inland we drove through the Western Highlands. There are acres of newly planted trees here. We also stopped in a ravine with the steep rocks around and the cold, icy, clear water stream flowing along. We cupped our hands and drank the refreshing water. We pushed on and parked at the foot of Ben Nevis. Climbing a sandy stoned path we made our way almost half the way up. Sitting on a stone with Ben Nevis in the background, Steve and I took it in turns to be photographed with mum. Mum wanted to walk all the way up but we persuaded her that it was time to find a hotel for the night. We made our way to Fort William and stayed in a beautiful hotel, although I must admit it was run a little like Faulty Towers but it certainly made for good entertainment. Our last day in Scotland we drove down and through Glasgow and pushed on down to Gretna Green. We visited the Old Blacksmith's shop where people used to elope to and get married in. We purchased a postcard of an old marriage certificate saying, 'The Kingdom of Scotland County of Dumfries, Parish of Gretna'. Opposite is the Lovers Leap Hotel. Mum remembered receiving a postcard from her firstborn son from Gretna Green declaring he had eloped and got married. So we took mum to the local Register Office, giving the name and date. We were given the register that our eldest brother had signed some 30 years previously. It was the first time mum had seen it and she shed a tear. Well, we crossed back into England and everybody agreed that this had been a super trip, fantastic scenery, great people and lots of fun.

GUERNSEY - CHANNEL ISLANDS, HERM, JERSEY

This is one place I have visited on many occasions and loved every trip and still always discover something new. It started when my sister worked the holiday season. She fell in love with the island and also a local fella called Dave. They went on to set up their own bed and breakfast and run it. So my first trip over was by ship. I love the old harbour area of St Peter Port, with all the boats tied up and the clinking of wire against the masts and at nighttime the cute little lights around the harbour, and the moon makes it a romantic setting. Sis's B&B was way up the top and I will never forget those steep inclines or multitude of steps, but the view from the top is splendid. On the coastline you can always find a secluded cove or a stretch of sandy beach uninhabited.

The history of the islands shows at one time during the Second World War that the German Nazis occupied the island. Still in existence are the many pillboxes and look-out points surrounding the coastline. I found the war museum fascinating, with a film showing parts of the occupation and mementoes from that era including uniforms, guns, ammunition, badges and photographs.

There is a fine shopping centre with markets of fresh fruit, flowers and vegetables. Also a fish market and, if you get your timing right, you can watch local fishermen bring their catches of the day in.

Once I took a two-week holiday here. A guest of my sister and Dave, another brother of mine, Cliff, and his wife Janet were staying there at the same time. We took many outings and excursions. One was to the island of Herm, which is a small island with lots of character. The beaches have soft sand and it is very peaceful here. No transport is allowed on the island except for an old tractor I saw. Other islands nearby are Sark and Alderney.

One of the best trips to Guernsey was for the marriage of my sister Virginia to Dave. Having most of the family there was brilliant. We all stayed in one hotel and had hired cars. The wedding took place in a lovely old church, the organ player used to drop a few notes as we sang *All Creatures Great and Small*. And we cried with laughter listening to brother Bill's singing voice. But apart from this, sis looked great and it was a superb day for everybody. The following day all the brothers played golf and for lunch we found a pub with an old wooden skittles alley. It was great fun having the family eat and play together just like it was when I was growing up. One night, John, Bill, Steve, Alan and myself were going to stay up and watch a football match. Alan's wife-to-be insisted that Alan stay with her in their room. About half an hour had gone by. For a laugh I telephoned Alan's room. Alan answered and I said, 'Spurs have scored.' He shouted back, 'So have I.' We fell about hysterical. We all had a brilliant time.

WHAT A WAY TO TRAVEL

On one of the trips by ship on the return journey we stopped at the island of Jersey, at St. Helier port. Mum, Steve and I walked down the gangplank and stood on the concrete dock, jumping up and down and kissing the ground. We claim we have been to Jersey. Now I know this is a super island so I plan to visit again one day. Also I have got to return to Guernsey. For one reason, my sister, niece and brother-in-law live here. Two, I have not seen the little church covered in shells and three, I love the place and there is still more to discover and enjoy.

FRANCE - PARIS / ANDORRA / SPAIN / PORTUGAL - LISBON - THE ALGARVE / SPAIN - SEVILLE – GIBRALTAR / MOROCCO - TANGIERS, RABAT, CASABLANCA

Steve and I booked a coach trip down to Lisbon, Portugal. However, we knew that the coach we caught out of London would drop us in Paris and another coach would take us through to Lisbon. What we did not know and had not been told was the pick-up point was the other side of Paris from where we were to be dropped. We arrived in Paris at five o'clock in the morning on a cold and wet summer day. We went into the Metro underground station to get warm and to keep dry. Not much was open and in any case we only had a fifty-franc note between us. We had no need of French money as the coach left at 10 am, and we had brought our own drinks with us. Steve only brought the note as a last minute thing for emergencies only. Well, the next three hours just dragged by, waiting for the coach station to open. It finally did at about 8.15 am. A queue soon formed. We waited awhile and then decided to check in. The guy behind the counter spoke very little English. All I could understand was

WHAT A WAY TO TRAVEL

'No, no, no, not here'. I went back to Steve and said, 'There's something wrong here.' Collecting my thoughts I went back to the counter. This time the guy was very sharp and aggressive with me but I persisted until he produced a Metro map and pointed out the nearest station and I got him to write down the address. Going back to Steve we had a decision to make. Do we stick it our here and find somebody who can explain just what is going on or do we take the gamble and head off on the Metro? Due to the time allowance we had to get it right. We gambled on the Metro. Moving swiftly out of the coach station and running through the many corridors of the Metro we arrived at the ticket counter, panting. Our map had shown us we had to go 27 stations and change at three stations. We had no room for an error as time was ticking away and we still had to find the coach station at the other end. We approached the lady at the ticket counter, pointed to the station on the map and asked for deux tickets. We gave her the fifty-franc note, approximate value £5:00. She said, 'No, no, no.' No change. We pointed to our wristwatch and said, 'Time, emergency.' She just nodded her head. 'No, no, no.' I looked at Steve. 'What are we going to do?' I asked. 'Give it a couple of minutes.' A few people came and went so I approached her again. Again she nodded, 'No,' I said to Steve, 'We'll have to jump the barrier somehow and risk it.' What happened next I can only explain as a miracle or somebody watching over us. As I stood there trying to work out a way through the revolving barrier a guy went to go through. All I remember about him was that he was wearing a white hat and carrying a rucksack. He then handed me two tickets. I turned to Steve and said, 'Steve, this bloke has given us two tickets.' As I turned back he had totally disappeared. Steve asked, 'What bloke?' I replied, 'The guy with the hat.' I had not even thanked him and he said nothing at all. We rushed through the barrier and tried to catch him but we never saw him again. We wondered if we had the correct tickets to the right value. There was only one way to find out. So we boarded the train, the tickets must have been all right because on two separate occasions ticket inspectors got on and checked our tickets. At the other end we ran to the coach station and were relieved when we had booked in. We checked our watches to find we only had ten minutes to spare. So everything worked out well, but who was that guy? Did he pay for the tickets? We just do not know the answers and probably never will, but we send him our heartfelt thanks and wish him all the best and good luck.

For the next two days everything calmed down. All we had to do was to sit back and relax and watch the scenery go by out of the coach window. Steve and I had the back seat so we could stretch out. There was plenty of room on the coach. It had its own toilet and we had bought plenty of food and drink so when we were not eating or drinking we were resting, sleeping or talking. They also showed us two video films and we frequently stopped to stretch our legs or top up our food and drink. We drove right down through France and crossed into Portugal, hugging the coastline before eventually entering the capital of Portugal – Lisbon. The entire trip passed so quickly and we thoroughly enjoyed it. The scenery to view was magic and was forever changing. We have a couple of great photographs lying

WHAT A WAY TO TRAVEL

there relaxing and one of Steve asleep and the two of us drinking out of our plastic coke containers with flexible straw extension.

Well, we got up a little stiff but found a hotel near to the coach station. While there we booked our ticket for the next leg of the journey. The coach leaves at 8 am tomorrow morning so that night we went out and had a good pizza, which was our first hot food for three days. And a beer. We walked around the city streets but wanted an early night and our first sleep in a bed for a few days.

On the way out of Lisbon we were lucky to catch a glimpse of the famous statue to the monument of the discoveries. Also travelling over the high bridge we got an incredible view of the city plus the statue of Christ with the arms outstretched as though blessing the whole city. We were treated to coffee on board and after only four hours we were travelling along the coastline of the Algarve. Our stop point was Albufeira. As we got off of the coach our first impression was that of a white oasis, as most of the buildings and hotels were white. We walked through the open market then through the town until finally reaching the beach wall. There in front of us was a fantastic beach of soft golden sand, warm, gently rippling sea, to the left and right sandy cliffs and it was a clear sky and the sun shone brightly. People in their swimsuits and half swimsuits mingled everywhere, sunbathing, strolling along or playing games on the beach. This is it, after those days on the coach. Now we had fresh sea breeze air and we knew we were going to enjoy ourselves in this place. All we needed now was a bit of luck getting booked into a hotel. To the right-hand side way up on top of the cliff a white building stood and it looked like a hotel. There were steps from the beach leading up to it. We decided to investigate it. If we were unlucky, well the least we could do was enjoy the view from the top of the steps. We trundled across the beach and past an enormous sand mound weathered by time. Reaching the top of the steep winding steps we were shattered, but what a view spanning right over the whole area. It was marvellous and well worth the effort of the climb. The white building was in fact a hotel, so we entered. The decoration was first-class and so were the prices. We told the guy that we just wanted three nights but that the price was outside of our budget. Totally rejected and feeling disappointed we went to walk away. 'Excusi,' he said, 'I have a private villa, you take a lookie. If you like it you take it. Much cheaper than the hotel but you must get and prepare you own food, OK?' We said that we would have a look. He made a quick call and sent us up the road about 100 yards.

There waiting for us was a little old lady dressed in black with a walking stick. She took us through the villa's front door. What was inside 'gob smacked' us. We were lost for words. We quickly said, 'Yes' to the old lady and gave her the agreed amount. She gave us the key and left. Steve and I danced around the villa, shouting, 'Yes, yes, yes.' The place was magnificent with marbled tiled floor, massive bedroom with two single beds and a wardrobe, a lounge area with blue settees, an ultra gleaming white bathroom with running hot water, a kitchen area with all the mod cons, cooker, fridge, pots and pans, a dining area and a door which led out onto our own balcony with a white table sunshade and chairs to match. Talk about landing on your feet. This was pure luck and magic. If I was a millionaire I could not buy a place as good as this. To top it off we can make as much mess as we like because a cleaner comes in every morning and cleans up. Yeah ha!! We knew we would love this place and, oh boy, what a good start we have had. We quickly changed into our swimsuits and headed for the beach. There were enough sunrays to catch in the afternoon to give us our first layer. Wrong. We fell asleep on the beach and became as red as lobsters. For the next three days that is all we did, lazing around the beach, swimming in the sea, looking at and talking to the topless girls. We used to take walks right along the shoreline, paddling in the water. We found a café right up the end of the beach, which served super coffee. By night we would stroll around the town. It is ever so picturesque, with its cobbled streets together with many bars and restaurants. We found a huge pineapple-looking plant, which made for a great photograph, standing under it. Sometimes we ate out and other times in. One night in the villa we cooked pizza, beans and sausages and quite often you would find us on our balcony catching the late sunrays of the day, playing cards and drinking beer. We bought some super postcards. One half was of three women in the 1890s in bathing suits, the other half three women in the 1990s. What a difference. Plus pictures of beach bums and girls emerging from the sea topless. But my favourite was of a very large lady with her back to the camera with the caption, 'I have found the nudist beach.'

On our last night in Albufeira we celebrated with whiting and chips for our dinner. We took in a lambada live music bar, had a few drinks and played pool on a circular round table, which was different to what we were used to. This is definitely a place to visit again as it has got a mixture of everything and well worth a stay. We have to push on; catching a local bus we follow the coastline. This gave me mixed feelings but on the one hand you had the beautiful alcoves, the jaded cliffs and little sandy bays which give the Algarve its unique coastline and the reason for people coming to the Algarve. On the other hand so many hotels and landscape complexes are going up in the whole area and its natural beauty is being destroyed. We carried on down to Faro, which is basically an old shopping town. We pushed on and finally reached Vila Real de Santo António, which is the border point before entering into Spain. We booked into a very old hotel but only three weeks ago complete renovation had taken place. The room was immaculate and the bathroom pristine and ultra white. We even took a photograph of it. Must be cracking up, taking photographs of loos. Steve thought the switch he pulled was a light. It was not, in actual fact it was the emergency alarm. The telephone rang and the door was knocked, checking out that we were all right. Mind you, it is one way of getting a drink during the evening. We strolled the streets and ate a huge pizza. We found a super signpost with Portugal across it and posed underneath for our photograph. We also purchased a lighter and a great big cockerel, as this is the symbol of Portugal. Next morning we caught the local ferry into Spain: forgetting the clocks go forward one hour we missed our scheduled bus. After a lengthy delay we eventually made it to

Seville and gained an amazing bonus for this year in Seville – it was EXPO 92 exhibition.

The exhibition centre took up a vast area and along the river we could see the replica ships identical to those sailed in by Christopher Columbus to find the new lands. This year being the 500th anniversary we purchased a postcard of the ships, showing in great detail the building and structure of the ships. Sometimes Steve and I feel like explorers discovering new lands, people, sights and cultures.

Well, the last train had left this evening for Gibraltar so we had the option of staying in Seville for the night, and most hotels would be full due to the exhibition, or negotiating a good price with a taxi driver to drive us all of the way. The Spanish driver wanted £125. We stuck to our guns and insisted on £85. Eventually, 'Del Monte he say 'Yes', or *Si*. The drive was to take three hours but then the driver had to turn around and come all the back again. The ride was fascinating, what with his vocabulary of English and mine of Spanish we attempted to speak about every subject, families, football and anything that moved. He kept on saying, 'Toro Toro.' I did not understand him until we turned a corner and saw a huge sign of a bull, and basically that summed up our conversation. Mind you, he did buy us a cup of coffee and he gave us his address in case we got into any trouble. He dropped us right on the border between Spain and Gibraltar. We bid him 'Adios, amigo,' and 'Gracias,' and he disappeared into the night. It was now 10 pm and customs and passport control awaited us. It was amazing to see short-sleeved English-dressed bobbies, especially from where we had just come from. But then, this is British territory. We walked over the surface of the road, which looked like an air runway strip. It was not until the next day that we realised it was. We were just pleased that no planes were landing at the time. We did not worry for long because there in front of us was the majestic Rock of Gibraltar. The outline could be clearly defined even in the darkness of the night. We walked on to the town centre, stopping en route for some good old fish and chips eaten out of newspaper. The town seemed to be buzzing with youngsters, darkened car windows and sunroofs were opened as music was being blasted out of them. Cars screeched to a stop or roared off into the night. We found a central hotel and hit the sack. Getting up early we had a full day planned. It was a beautiful day so we decided to walk right the way around the rock. It felt like a ten-mile walk and took just over two hours to complete but it was splendid all the way. With so many interesting things en route, first was to touch it. Its chalky walls were crumbling in some parts but in general it was as solid as a rock. Taking photographs straight up the steep side. We discovered an old aeroplane propeller mangled during the Second World War. We saw the Straits of Gibraltar, the start point of the Mediterranean Sea, with huge oil tankers going each way and anchored off shore. We also observed a British nuclear submarine and the old sewage pipes. The rock has a multitude of tunnels and caves from the outside. Many holes can be seen and it was said during the war that they acted as a unique defence system. You can also drive right through the rock. A hole has been dug right through the rock taking two-way traffic. We posed for a photograph in

WHAT A WAY TO TRAVEL

the great opening before disappearing into the semi-darkness, the fumes and the heavy rumble of traffic. It was good to emerge the other side. Once our ears stopped ringing and our eyes were adjusted to the light again, we walked past the many barrack homes to those military service people stationed on the rock, and the dry docks for shipbuilding. After this walk and heat to contend with it was time to put our feet up and take a well-deserved drink, but we had done it right around the rock and through it, and now we have got to go up it.

As we were studying the advertising board for the taxi guided rock tours, an oldish man named Jim approached us. He was an ex-patriot of Britain and had lived many years on Gibraltar. His knowledge of the rock and its history was first-class and he had a fascinating way of delivering it. With enthusiasm and accuracy. We could ask any question we liked and he always gave us a straight answer. He told us about the time that the border to Spain had been closed, about the visit of Winston Churchill during the war years and the visit in 1954 of Her Majesty Queen Elizabeth II and the Duke of Edinburgh. Then he took us way back in time and told us about Nelson and the Battle of Trafalgar and about the cemetery, which is here. He gave us the history of Gibraltar back to when the land was ruled by the Moors. He told us that Gibraltar had fourteen sieges in its history and England finally took the rock in 1704, which was then given by the Queen of Spain. The land had been ruled the longest by the Moors, then the English, then Spanish. The whole trip was to cost £21 for the two of us. It was worth it just for the knowledge he instilled into us. He told us about the government and how

WHAT A WAY TO TRAVEL

the voting was done, and their school system and what it took to emigrate from Britain here. And how one day he may return home. It was fascinating listening to him as we wound our way slowly up the rock. Reaching the top offered an incredible view of the surrounding area. We could see the whole of Gibraltar, the runway we had walked across last night. Jim told us of a story of an aeroplane landing. A motorcyclist ignored the barrier warnings and flashing lights. Carrying on, he was hit and killed by the aeroplane coming in. We could see Spain to the left and to the right the Mediterranean Sea and Africa. Jim pointed out the mountain, which in mythology is said Hercules stood one foot on that mountain and one foot on the rock: parting the land he formed the Mediterranean Sea. We then went deep inside the rock and saw incredible rock formations weathered over the years by running water. From the ceiling hung incredible stalactites and from the floor upwards stalagmites. Lights had been added to give the walls a magnificent colour spectacle. A stage had been erected for shows, especially singing, as the acoustics were incredible. Back outside we read up on Winston Churchill's visit and photographed the famous 'V' sign he used to use. And we fed, played and photographed the famous Barbary apes. Churchill said so long as the apes were on the rock, the rock would always be British. During the war special food parcels were flown in to feed the apes. We watched and photographed the cable car coming and going. We saw the plaque to commemorate the Queen's visit in 1954, saying this was the spot they actually stood on and looked out over Gibraltar, and I was standing on the same spot. We also saw the magnificent guns at the top, old and recent. An old cannon stood there, a relic from the ancient days gone by. It was great standing next to it with my hand on its barrel and Gibraltar docks in the background. On the way back down from the rock Jim stopped at his friend's souvenir shop. We purchased some fantastic postcards of satellite photographs showing the size of the rock in relation to the land area of Gibraltar. Other purchases, a lighter with three apes on covering their eyes, ears and mouth, plus an ornament of a mother ape and her young with 'Gibraltar' on the platform. What a superb day we had. We thanked Jim and told him we would meet him in London one day. Exhausted, an early night was on the cards, plus we are up at 7 am tomorrow.

AFRICA - MOROCCO - TANGIER - RABAT - CASABLANCA

After a quick breakfast we took a taxi down to the ferry port. It was mayhem down there. A large queue for tickets had already formed but it was the mound of luggage that amazed us. Boxes, packages and holdalls, but it was still no problem getting our ticket.

£14 one way for a three-hour crossing. We meet some interesting people on the crossing who told us some history, cultures and information about the country we were about to visit. On the last leg of the journey we went outside on the ferry and watched the start of the African coastline as it got nearer and nearer. Getting off of the ferry, however, was harder than getting on. The local Moroccan people gathered in a hoard

WHAT A WAY TO TRAVEL

waiting to pounce the moment that you set foot off of the gangway. 'Taxis', 'A hotel,' 'Carry your bags' were screamed at you, plus pulling of your clothes, tugging on your arm and even picking up your cases. We stayed towards the back and let most of the crowd gets their bookings. With a deep breath we took the plunge. Steve and I had decided we did not need a guide, as we would find our own hotel and way around. So by keeping on walking, looking straight ahead and saying, 'No thank you,' we kept moving. However, one local Moroccan was very persistent. He followed us for over 200 yards, asking where we were going, what we needed or wished to see. We were as polite as possible but firm in our 'No's. Eventually he produced a badge with his photograph on saying he was not a guide but a government official. His only desire was to make sure we had a good time in his country, to see everything we wanted to see and to be safe. Even if it was a pack of lies, it sounded good. I said to Steve, 'Let's give this guy a go.' He agreed so we told him first thing was to unload our bags. Even the locker room was scary. He told the guy behind the counter that he wanted our bags looked after and not to be tampered with. He got us to carry with us our passport and money. Then we needed to change our money into local currency. So he took us to a bank with a very good exchange rate. 'What next?' he asked. We told him that we wanted to soak up the atmosphere of the local market and browse amongst the local arts and crafts, then sample a local dish for lunch. 'Leave it to me,' he said. 'Follow me, but stay close.' And off we went. First visit was the open congested market, an explosion of colour, smells and

WHAT A WAY TO TRAVEL

activity. Amongst the many tents and canvases was a multitude of gold shining dishes, pots and pans, jugs, bowls and vases. There were piles of heaped dough bread, trays of spices, nuts and beans, fresh fruit and jewellery in abundance. But the whole place had a unique air about it. Apart from the splendid odours there was bustling and jostling, bartering and an excitement in the air. The dress of the people added to the uniqueness of the market. Many different types of coloured robes and headgear but above all the faces and smiles, the warm friendly handshakes and the willingness to exchange ideas and stories and corners of the market. He kept the persistent shopkeepers at bay and the beggars at arm's distance. He kept us moving and took us to a carpet storehouse. We were made welcome immediately and given a refreshing mint tea. Carpet after carpet was rolled out in front of us. Incredible textures and colours, sheer quality and craftsmanship, but the real punch was trying to say 'No'. They used every trick in the book. I think 'No' to them meant 'Yes' really. We tried, 'No, no, no,' but they still though that meant, 'Yes, yes, yes.'

I thought the only way out of this was to tell a few jokes. I told a few camel jokes and had them rolling about with laughter. They kept shaking our hands and saying, 'Very good, now which one do you want?' But we thanked them for their time and moved towards the exit. Reaching the outside we let out a blast of air. Our guide told us we had not seen anything yet and took us down the road to the souvenir shop, telling us when we could not take any more to call for him and he would get us out of there. Well, it all started well, another nice glass of mint tea. Then the Moroccan robes were put over us plus a fez was placed on our heads. We looked superb, just like the locals. We photographed each other walking around the shop. We were having such a laugh doing our Tommy Cooper impersonations, but getting them off was another story. You definitely needed assistance and they were not willing to help. All they kept doing was lowering the price. The price came down so much Steve was very tempted, but I asked him when back home would he ever wear it? He agreed, but also had trouble trying to get it off. Wandering around the store we saw many knives, daggers and swords and an incredible selection of leather items, belts, bags, shoes and slippers. We, however, settled for a pair of Moroccan dolls dressed in full national costume and a small sabre with cover and 'Morocco' printed on it. Steve decided to buy the fez he was wearing, providing they helped us out of the robes. Before disrobing us they gave us one more final price but we stood our ground and said 'No' for the umpteenth time.

Next stop was food time. He took us to a traditional Moroccan restaurant. Entering through small archways we were in a darkened room lit only by flickering candles. We were taken to the far side of the room where opposite was a three-piece band. Their instruments included a violin, bongos and a sort of guitar with bent stem and domed base. We sat down and were given our mint tea while we decided on what to eat. Our guide suggested the traditional Moroccan dish of couscous, a soup starter of meat and vegetables followed by rice, chicken and vegetables, finished with a dessert of cake with pieces of chicken in it. Throughout the meal the band played Moroccan

WHAT A WAY TO TRAVEL

tunes while the belly dancer did her twists, turns and rumblings. Our guide stayed with us at the table and told us his life story. His nickname being Chicago Joe, he was an ex-boxer. No wonder nobody gave him any trouble in the market. He told us about his family and way of life and how much he loved his job, and stories about people he would meet while doing his job. What a scene to remember – good food, a fine setting, unusual music, exotic dancing and good company. On the way out we wanted to photograph the band and dancer. They invited us to sit with them. We jumped at the opportunity. They put the fez hats on our heads and gave us an instrument each. Chicago Joe took the photographs and they developed brilliantly. We told Joe of our plans. We wished to get as far as Casablanca. He told us of a train, which would take us there today, but it leaves at 16.00 hours, just two hours' time. We had a decision to make. Do we stay here and catch another train or push on forward? We considered what a marvellous day we had so far and there was no way to top it. Plus we had seen and done everything we had wanted. 'Joe,' we said, 'Take us to the train station.' Via the lockers, rucksacks all in order, we thanked Joe for our wonderful day. 'All part of the service,' he said. 'What about a tip?' we asked. 'No, no,' he answered, 'All part of the service. How much were you thinking about?' he asked. We all agreed an amicable price. He was good at his job but I actually think he enjoyed our company as well. We did make him laugh. Joe helped us get our tickets. We shook his hand and parted company and he disappeared into the crowd.

When we first arrived on the platform it was completely empty

WHAT A WAY TO TRAVEL

but over the next two hours everybody and anybody joined us, coming up to the last ten minutes before the train arrived. The platform was ten-deep in people and the whole length of the station, and that is not to mention the luggage they had with them. They had bundles, packages, boxes and cases. Steve and I said to each other, 'When the train pulls in just go for it. First one on saves a seat for the other'. Just then a porter walked by. He smiled, stopped and asked, 'Where are you from?' 'London, England,' we informed him. He told us he had a friend who lived in London, near Buckingham Palace, named John. We asked if his last name was Major. He roared with laughter and said that he would look after us. When the train pulls in he would be jumping on it early and to watch out for him and he would signal to us and then we could make a beeline for him. We said OK and he disappeared into the crowd. As the train approached, mayhem struck everybody. People were diving onto the train and hauling themselves up before the train had even stopped. People were literally hanging off of the train and when it finally came to a standstill a stampede for seats began. We were nearly squashed to a pulp. Then I saw the porter waving frantically out of a window. Steve and I fought our way to the carriage he was in. As I got to the doorway a large woman was trying to get up the steps. She was sort of stuck in the doorway. I placed my hands strategically on her behind and pushed. She went through like a cork out of a champagne bottle. We eventually reached the carriage with the porter in. He had saved us two seats right by the window. OK, it had cost us around £5 but it was well worth it just to be on the train – the bonus was the seat. As we looked out of the window the people had formed human chains to pass the baggage and bundles on. It was like watching organised chaos. In our compartment there were quite a mixed bag of people. A couple of twenty-year-old young men. The large lady I had helped to board the train and her husband and a separate older man and woman, the older man taking his shoes off immediately and, my God, his feet really stunk. The large lady started to eat straight away and the younger men struck up a conversation with us. Exchanging cigarettes, they asked us where we were headed for. We informed them that it was Casablanca and they asked, 'Why?' We told them because of the name itself. I love the sound of Casablanca and you can ask people if they have ever visited Casablanca and the majority says that they have not. Even ask them what country it is in and most people will not know, despite the fact they have heard of or seen the famous film. The second reason is that we wanted to see some of the country and experience the culture further south. They told us that Casablanca was just a city and that if we really wanted to see their country we were invited to get off of the train when they did and stay in their homes in the hills and see the real Moroccan way of life. The offer was too good to miss. We agreed with enthusiasm that we would, but as the trip went by we realised we would be in the middle of nowhere and nobody would even know where we had gone to, so at the last minute we declined. They were none too happy and even swore at us, which made us realise that we had made the right decision. They got off of the train and we went on to Rabat, the capital of Morocco. We only had a few minutes on the station platform before the train moved off for Casablanca. We arrived at 23.00 hours.

At this time of night in a strange city and not knowing where you are or where you want to go to, not speaking the language and with no maps, the best thing you can do is to find a hotel quickly. This is definitely a cosmopolitan city. I thought it would be a place in the outback but it is a thriving metropolis. Many of the hotels near to the station are either four or five star and our budget had nearly evaporated. Whilst walking around the city streets we get a real feeling for the place. That feeling when you know you are going to enjoy yourself. All we need now is a little bit of luck for a bed for the night and there it is, we hoped. Right between the skyscrapers and grand hotels was a two star hotel. Well, two blobs actually, but for seven pounds a night it was right up our street and had room. We booked in, dumped our bags and crossed the road to a roadside café, which was still open. We celebrated reaching our final destination with food and drink and for the next hour watched the people coming and going. It was a beautiful warm evening with a clear sky and you could see every star above. The night we slept well, taking breakfast in the café opposite, and we set out to explore the city.

Very nearby was a local market and it was fun exploring it at a more leisurely pace than that in Tangiers. All local arts and crafts were on display and we never got hassled so much. If we did we told them three words Chicago Joe had taught us and it worked every time. They just walked away from us. We had lunch in a pastry shop and ordered what looked like a sausage roll, but when you bit into it, it was red hot with some sort of

WHAT A WAY TO TRAVEL

chilli paste. So we just ate the pastry. The afternoon we spent strolling around the many shops and photographed a traditional water seller with his cask and cups and decorative clothing. We also stumbled across some amazing postcards showing the Sahara desert, which was not that far away. Also pictures of local tribesmen on horseback riding with their guns in the air and one of an incredibly beautiful belly dancer. We went back down to the station because it was the only place we could find a sign with Casablanca on. So we stood underneath it for our photograph with the name above. Another super photograph was the entrance to a hotel with rich, thick carpets laid on the ground with the swing door and two white pillars outside and above an amazing archway of a typical Moroccan-style architecture with a hanging lamp. We actually looked so small standing inside the archway. That evening we spent most of the night sitting outside on the street in front of the café opposite the hotel. We mixed with the locals and just observed what was going on around us. Shoe cleaners, cigarette sellers, belts, and sunglasses. They all approached us. One chap even got off of his motorbike. He was wearing a suit and tie. He was trying to sell us something. He had assumed that we were English and went on mumbling about something. When he received no answers to his questions he asked us where we have come from. As quick as a flash I answered Czechoslovakia. He look absolutely stunned and said that he could speak nine different languages but not Czechoslovakian. So he shook our hands and left. Steve turned to me and said in a Humphrey Bogart voice, 'In all the bars in all the lands he had to come into ours.' I turned

WHAT A WAY TO TRAVEL

to Steve and in the same voice said, 'Play it again, Steve.' We both cracked up. The next day we packed our bits up and flew home to England. The end of another adventure.

ACROSS EUROPE FRANCE / GERMANY / CZECHOSLOVAKIA - PRAGUE / AUSTRIA - VIENNA

BRATISLAVA/HUNGARY - BUDAPEST/YUGOSLAVIA/ DENMARK - COPENHAGEN/SWEDEN - MALMO

Travelling across France and Germany by coach we reached Czechoslovakia after touring through the night and a 23-hour ride. We arrived in Prague at 7 am feeling shattered from our interrupted sleep and in need of a good stretch along with food and drink. We took a walk and went in search of food and drink. We found a café with many of the locals inside so assumed it must be of good standard. Hence why it was popular. Now, you have got to remember this is 7.30 in the morning. Most of the regulars were drinking beer; this includes men and women. They were tucking into dishes of soup, spaghetti bolognese, meat sandwiches and an assortment of bread and cheeses. We settled for cake and coffee. Fully recharged, it was time for our city tour of Prague. Prague has been named the city of a thousand spires and is rich in magnificent architecture, baroque domes, golden cupolas, renaissance palaces and majestic spires. It is like visiting a city from the 18th century. The river Vltava threads its way through the city. Crossing the river you find yourself in the old town of Stare Mesto with its fascinating medieval alleyways and lively shopping streets. Wander through to Wenceslas Square, the heart of old Prague. We found a tourist bus and on the back it said 'Welcome Praha'. We posed next to it for a photograph. Also we stood outside a bank for a photograph because of the word above, CESKOSLOVENSKA, the local spelling. Another photograph we took was of a dome. Just below was a semi-circle with a beautifully painted picture on it. The old colourful Burghers' houses blend so well together and we noticed although the city had not changed much over the centuries the people, however, were starting to change to Western ways in clothing and fashions. Although still keeping their own unique identity, the changes were slowly taking place. The best evidence of that were things for sale in the open markets, shops and roadside stalls. Although Prague is a lovely place we were so near to a place I had dreamed of going to for years. We booked a coach, which was to be leaving at 15.00, and this was to go to Vienna. So we had just over an hour to enjoy Prague. Our final photograph was next to an advertisement board for McDonalds, showing there were four available, and a map of the area and 'Prague' in large red letters. We looked a bit dishevelled after our trip through the night, our clothes were wrinkled and we were unwashed and unshaved. With our last Koronas we purchased a few postcards, a snack and drink, then we left for a four-hour coach ride. Just before leaving Czechoslovakia we stopped for a rest break. Taking this opportunity, we though we would use the toilet. Entering through the men's door a little old lady sat behind a counter.

WHAT A WAY TO TRAVEL

As we came through she shook her little jug at us with a few coins in it and mumbled a few words. Steve and I had no notes or change at all so it was a race to get out. First I made it. When I went out she was screaming and shouting. By the time Steve left she was on her feet, waving her arms around and going mad. We were glad to get back on the coach and cross the Austrian border. We arrived in Vienna just after 19.00 hours.

AUSTRIA - VIENNA

At last I have got here. For years I had seen and heard so much about Vienna which gave me the urge to one day stand on its historical streets, admire the buildings and architecture and to sample the music and atmosphere. It is renowned the world over. Today is that day, but we had arrived with no Austrian schillings so we needed a hotel that would either change our money for us or allow us to pay tomorrow. Over the next couple of days there is a conference in town so many hotels were fully booked. Those that did have vacancies were over a hundred pounds per night. So we kept on walking, twisting and turning down different side streets and alleyways. This is a huge city and well spread out. We had no map or directions. We just kept strolling, taking in the sights and sounds, until we reached a river. We thought it was the Danube and we found out later that it was just an inlet from the Danube. But between the inlet and the Danube away from the city centre we found an amazing array of small restaurants, bars and cafés. Dotted in between were smaller hotels and we knew we had struck gold. We kept looking and eventually found an ideal hotel. We went inside and just needed a little bit of luck now. They only had one room available for the night and would they change our money? No, it was too late. Could we pay tomorrow? No problem. We were in. Brilliant. The guy was so helpful, too. He gave us a map of the area. We told him all the things we wanted to see and he marked them on the map for us. We dumped our bags upstairs and went back to a small tavern we had seen on the way in. Downing a large cold lager we planned our tour for the following day. If only we could have booked in for two nights it would have been perfect. After the lager and last night's sleep our beds were sheer bliss. We slept like logs but we got up at the crack of dawn, showered and shaved. Today was going to be fun-packed and hectic. There is just so much to do and see. Breakfast was superb; orange drink, then a self-service selection of cheese, ham and other meats, boiled eggs, rolls, toast, bread, croissants, Ryvitas, jams, peaches and as much coffee as you could drink. That set us up for the day. I went to reception to explain that we were going to change our money, then return and pay. I just happened to ask if there had been any cancellations. She replied that there had and one room was available that night. I shouted that we would take it and I was advised that we would have to change rooms. It was no problem and we would do it now. After another stroke of luck like this we knew this was going to be a superb day. Leaving the hotel we caught a local tram back into the city. First job was to exchange our money. Now it was time just to enjoy such a splendid city. Our start point right in the centre was St Stephen's cathedral. Over 800 years old. Going inside, although darkened, it gave off warmth and a feeling of historic times coupled with the fact of the millions of people who had gone before you. Some were so famous the world knew their names. Steve and I felt so humble so we decided to light a candle and place it in the rack and we prayed and gave thanks for being looked after on our travels and we acknowledged the patron saint of travel, St Christopher. Reaching the outside and your eyes adjusting to the light there were thousands of people milling about from all over the world going every which way. The square with its cobbled stone floor was a beehive of activity. People in groups were singing, two girls dressed in long silk coats and wearing white wigs resembling the fashion of the days gone by were selling tickets for a performance by the Mozart orchestra. We had a lovely conversation with them and they gave us a sample ticket to keep.

Other people were taking horse-drawn carriages around the maze of small streets. We, however, were in search of a famous house. None other than that of Mozart. We walked through many alleyways, cobbled streets and squares. Some of the alleyways had beautifully decorated emblems over the entrance. My favourite, which we photographed, was of an old chap wearing a hat and holding a glass in his hand. He was appearing out of a window frame with his smiling face and he appeared to be toasting you. On the wall next to him were meats, chicken and fruit, obviously advertising food and drink. We also encountered a mannequin dressed like the girls in the square with coat and wig. As we posed for a photograph I could not help but stretch my hand out as though we were about to shake hands. Eventually we found the house. Standing there looking up at the tiny windows, it is said Mozart wrote some of his finest works from this address. We wondered what sort of neighbours he had and did they ever complain about the noise from next door. The house is now a museum devoted to his memory. The buildings, structures and statues are something else here. For one thing they're everywhere, almost on every building. Secondly they are magnificent in design and creativity and they are so accessible. You can get close to them, touch them and be part of them. So it was time to snap away with the camera. One of the snaps you could sit on the edge of a water fountain. Above you in brilliant white lay four figures, their bodies twisted in all directions and at the top, standing on a boat, was a princess with one arm in the air. Another set of statues we found reminded us of Hercules' tasks. There were about seven structures of the same man figure, but either fighting or tussling with a beast with four heads and a club in his hands, or gripping a wild beast with sabah light protruding teeth. They would have made for super photographs and stand outside the Hofburg Palace. We went through the archway to the other side and surrounding area where there are many magnificent buildings with grand balconies, huge pillars and statues dotted along the rooftop. We were heading for my favourite – outside the parliament building, a statue of Athena the Greek goddess. It is truly magnificent. The backdrop is the parliament building with its many pillars and in front is the water fountain, which you sit on, to be in the picture. Behind you are five statues of men and a woman with a child. Either lying or sitting, one holds a sword, the other a paddle, the child has his hand in the running water, then in the centre is a column and on it she stands. She holds a spear in her left hand, the metal point being finished in gold colour. She has a gold-coloured chest piece and gold-coloured head crown but in her right hand she holds what I can only describe as a small black angel with wings. I found the whole structure to be breathtaking. It is just a marvellous piece of art and it is not even in a gallery or museum. It is on the streets for everybody to see, touch, enjoy and be photographed with.

I believe if you ask anybody about Vienna, one thing springs to their mind and that has to be music. This is a city where Mozart, Beethoven, Haydn, Mahler, Schubert, Brahms and the Strausses found inspiration. Where orchestras still play the beloved symphony and people still dance to the Viennese waltz. So we went in search of the Stadtpark where monuments to the great composers are remembered. Catching a tram, we nearly missed the park. The statues are very hidden between the wooded tree-lined park.

Once in the park, it is a marvellous setting. Well-mown grass, beautiful hanging trees and an abundance of beautiful flowerbeds with an array of colourful flowers. One set of yellow pansies formed a musical note. We photographed the monuments with the famous names finished in gold-coloured lettering. The most picturesque monument has to be that of Johann Strauss, an archway decorated with figurines, and on a small stem just in front of the arch is a golden statue of Strauss playing the violin. It looks splendid with a bed of flowers in front. We walked up and touched the golden figure representing a genius of his time. By the time we had finished our tour the daylight was coming to an end. The night scene took on a different atmosphere. Street performers were on every corner, some doing mime theatre, others had a violin or guitar and played classical tunes that you could recognise and tap your feet along to. Other people were wearing their best suits and gowns for a night out on the town, perhaps either to one of the restaurants or bars, or simply a night of music and dancing. We, however, had such an eventful and exhilarating day that we decided on a pizza and beer in a quaint little restaurant near to the hotel. The rest of the night we spent talking about our day and writing up our diaries of memoirs, sights and sounds, then we just crashed out.

The next day started with our super breakfast. We paid our hotel bill and with bags packed we were heading for the next leg of our trip. Our destination was Budapest in Hungary. Our opinion is that there is only one way to travel to Budapest and that is right down the Blue Danube on the water, following the twisting and winding river banks. We decided to take the hydrofoil so we had to get to the dock on the Danube. We had about a 3-mile walk but plenty of time on our hands as the sailing time was not until 15.00 hours. Strolling along on a beautiful day we were leaving Vienna with such happy memories. It had lived up to everything I would have expected and more. As we walked along we came across a theme park. Going in there was a multitude of rides and games. Also the famous big wheel ride which was used in one of the James Bond movies. The structure was of metal with huge carriage cars dotted on the outside, and over 14 viewing platforms. It was fascinating watching the people get in and out. The original structure was made entirely of wood but completely destroyed by fire. We visited the souvenir shop and purchased a tiny wooden violin with Wien (Vienna) on the front panel to remind me of the music of Vienna, also some splendid postcards, one of the great four, Mozart, Schubert, Beethoven and Strauss. It was strange looking into their faces and seeing how they are still being remembered. As we strolled through the theme park watching the children playing, a band struck up. They looked like toy soldiers. It was unrealistic. You had to follow the music. We left the theme park and headed for a local market. There we bought a bread roll, cheese, tomatoes, fruit and a drink. We had decided to take a picnic on the bank of the river Danube. On the way to the river we discovered a signpost saying Austria and Vienna Centre. Posing underneath it sort of summed up our whole trip with the impressive name. When we reached the river we were impressed by the width of it and the fact that the river was so fast-flowing and we could see for miles in each direction. The picnic was superb. Just eating, drinking and watching the river life. We stood posing by the river and photographed some of the passing boats. We even stuck our thumbs out as though hitching a ride. Then all of a sudden our hydrofoil pulled up alongside the bank. Now all we had to do was fight our way on and get the front two seats.

We made it to the front seats. The trip was about four and a half hours long. Right down the centre of the river Danube. As we sat there all of a sudden we floated away from the bank then the front end went up and off we went. It was a smooth ride with good vision out of the windows and, of course, it is one of the fastest methods to travel on water. The views along the river were of forest land, small little bays of white sand with nudists sunbathing along the whole stretch and so many water sports going on around you. There was always something to catch your eye or keep your attention. Every time we passed a boat, ship or hydrofoil coming the other way our boat sounded its siren, hooters and bells acknowledging the oncoming vessel. Occasionally we had to stop as wood or a branch of a tree would get wedged between the foils. At one point we approached a solid concrete wall. It was actually a lock. As we sat there the water steadily emptied away. The people on top looked so small as we slowly lowered with the water. Eventually a gap appeared between the concrete wall and the water, then these huge metal gates opened and we passed through, now being at the same level as the water. Further down the river on the banks were many historic castles and palaces from ancient times. We also pulled into Slovakia and the ancient capital of Bratislava but in general we kept moving and it was a very enjoyable ride. As we approached Budapest we had magnificent views; being as the water was so low down all our views were upwards. We passed under magnificent bridges until we reached our docking point. To our right-hand side was the old ancient town of Buda and to our left was the newer buildings of modern Pest.

HUNGARY - BUDAPEST

That is it, we had arrived and now stood on Hungarian soil in Pest. We walked through the brightly-lit shopping centre and streets. We were amazed as it was nothing like what we had expected. The streets, shops and restaurants were packed. We had always considered this to be an Eastern European country, a communist state behind the Iron Curtain. But we could not have been more wrong. The whole place was very westernised; the clothes that people wore were very fashionable. The women were outstanding and stunning, wearing short mini skirts, colourful tops and decorative jewellery. People walked the main street, posing and going places. The whole centre seemed to be alive and buzzing. Everything stayed open until late. We walked away from the centre to find a hotel to stay in. After about an hour of looking and enjoying the street scenery we stopped on a bus seat for a snack and drink. A guy was standing at the bus stop and we beckoned him over and asked him about hotels in the area. He had just returned from a trip to England and spoke perfect English. He told us there was only one hotel this side of the city but gave us loads of information about the area and places of interest to visit. His bus came so he had to go. We followed his directions and found the hotel. It was ideally situated for us and reasonable in price. We went in, only to be confronted by a very rude and aggressive receptionist. I would not exactly describe her as a model either, but we tried a 'Hello' that fell flat. We asked if there were any vacancies. She shouted back at us that the hotel was fully booked. We asked if we could book a room for the following night. 'No, no, no,' she screamed, 'We're all booked up.' So we left and stood outside the hotel on the street. We felt so disappointed, sort of let down, deflated. Our plans shattered, plus the fact it was beginning to grow dark. I sat down and had a smoke. Turning to Steve, I asked him to stay put as I was going back in.

Once inside the receptionist looked shocked to discover I had returned. I tried a different approach and started with a 'How are you?' Then I shot into pleading, telling her we were desperate. She looked at her book as I told her we would even sleep in the broom cupboard. Then, amazed, she said that they had a room although it was not a hotel room but a conference room split into two with two single beds. Without even seeing it I said that we would take it. I told her I would just go and get my brother, who was outside. She just nodded. Outside I approached Steve and told him to pick up his bags as we were in. He asked how, and what did I say? I told him I could not tell him now but would explain everything inside. He punched the night air with sheer delight, and then he shook my hand vigorously and said, 'Well done, Broth.' We went back in and I told the receptionist that Steve was the brother I told you about. Steve greeted her and got a 'Hello' back. She gave us a key and we went and got into the lift. Steve was so pleased and excited. He asked me to tell him all, as it was a miracle. I turned to him with a dead pan face and said I had told her that you would sleep with her tonight. His mouth just dropped open. It was so believable, what with her being so hard and the hotel fully booked. Steve fell for my gag, hook, line and sinker. Looking rather confused and serious I kept it up until we got inside the room. Then I just exploded with laughter. Once I had explained what his face had looked like and what had really been said, he said, 'What a relief,' and fell about laughing himself I think he must have thought it was a narrow escape. The room was ideal, comfortable, clean,

WHAT A WAY TO TRAVEL

with our own toilet and bath. On the wall were two sheepskins. We decided to go and get a beer and celebrate our luck. The streets were still very active. Nearby was an Opera House and showtime theatre. Everybody seemed to be coming out at the same time, which swelled the people on the pathways. We chose a bar where we could sit outside, have a beer and watch what was going on in the way of street life.

We slept well and went to breakfast. The only food we ate was hard-boiled eggs and dry white bread. We left the hotel and set off on foot for the old town of Buda. We crossed one of the many bridges spanning the river Danube separating Buda from Pest. In the middle we stopped for a photo shoot. Posing each side we took two photographs, one showing the old parliament building with the green dome of Buda and the other showing the high-rise buildings of modem Pest. We also took one looking right down the Danube with the bridges in the far distance. We carried on over the bridge and into the old town. It is totally different to that of Pest, with little cobbled streets and small wooden-framed houses. We worked our way up to the main train station and booked our next leg of the journey: a train ride through the rest of Hungary, crossing the border into Yugoslavia, then down to Belgrade through the rest of Yugoslavia, crossing the border into Bulgaria, going through Sofia which is the capital, then down to the Turkish border and finally on to our destination, Istanbul. We paid approximately £120 for two tickets one way and the train was leaving tomorrow morning at 6.10 a.m. We left the station and came across a brilliant sign in green saying 'Budapest Tourist'. We both stood next to it and pointed for our photographs. We caught a tram back to Pest and stopped off for lunch at a McDonald's with a difference. It was part of an old railway station converted into a restaurant with marbled floors and a high ceiling and tables on varying floor levels – quite splendid.

We headed back to the hotel to get our money to exchange to local currency to pay for our hotel bill, which we had booked for one extra night. Leaving the hotel we were heading for a legal exchange bureau when we were stopped in the street by a man asking if we wished to exchange money. Now, let me tell you, we never ever exchange money on the streets and these are the reasons. One, you set yourself up to be robbed by exposing where you keep your money. Two, it is against the law in many countries and you can get arrested for it. Three, quite often they will pass you old money which is no longer legal tender and therefore useless and fourth, I am just about to explain it to you is 'Greed'. Out of curiosity I asked him what exchange rate he was giving. It was obviously higher than that of the banks. I asked him how much we would get for 60 English pounds. He made his calculation and told us it was equivalent to 9,300. He had made a mistake as it should have been less, and that is when my greed took over. He said, 'Yes' and told us to follow him down a side street. He told Steve to be the look-out, which obviously took his attention away from what was about to happen. He then counted the 9,300 notes out in front of me and placed the 9,300 in my own hands and told me to check it. I physically counted it out and it was all there. And this is where the sting took place. He then took it back while I got my money out and counted it for him. He then placed a bundle of money into my hand, closing my fist around it, and advised me not to count it in the street. With that he thanked us, we thanked him and then parted company. We walked about 10 yards then I opened my hand to put the money into my wallet. All that was there were the 300, the 9,000 did not exist. He had switched it in the exchange. I cried out to Steve, 'He's done us.' Steve thought that I was joking. We ran back to the side street but he had already completely disappeared. He had gained himself time by telling us not to open my hand in the street. I felt sick, gutted and cheated. How could I have been so stupid, foolish and downright gullible? I thought that I was streetwise. I had travelled the world, seen and been told so many stories like this, and I had let it happen to me. What an idiot. But it also brought me down to earth. I had got to the point where I thought I knew everything, always thinking my ideas were best and right. This had taught me a huge lesson. I was human like everybody else and I also could make mistakes. Steve was absolutely brilliant about it all. I was so down on myself but he lifted my sprits and told me to put it down to experience. There was nothing we could do about it now and that it must not spoil the rest of our trip. I told him when we got back home I would give him his £30 back and he told me that I would not, as that money has gone and finished. We were both at fault. But it will never happen to us again. My last point on this is that guy could have completely destroyed our trip if we had not got any more money. OK, it probably helps him and his family to survive, but I can tell you if I had seen him again I would not have been able to control myself. I would have smashed his face in. That is how much it had affected me, I was furious.

Well, we did eventually get to exchange our money legally and pay our hotel bill. We had an early night, as we were to be up at 4 am in the morning. We checked out of the hotel and took a taxi to the train station. We had just enough Hungarian money left to purchase three tiny wooden dolls painted in traditional Hungarian costume and two coffees. We took a photograph of the train with a nameplate showing 'Budapest, Belgrade, Sofia and Istanbul'. I stood next to it showing six on my fingers, indicating six o'clock in the morning. We got on the train and had our own compartment. The train pulled out on time. We had an 18-hour journey ahead of us. We had purchased food for the journey, a loaf of bread, crisps, fruit, chocolate and a bottle of orange drink. The first three hours were magic. We talked about previous trips and made plans for when we reached Istanbul. We were so buzzed up, pleased to be leaving Budapest and excited about the train journey travelling through war-torn Yugoslavia and spending a few days in Istanbul. Then travelling down the west side of Turkey visiting Galipoli, Troy, Ephesus and Bodrum, then taking a local ferry to the Greek island of Kos, then across to Crete and finally to Malta and then home. As we were chatting away we noticed we were crossing the border between Hungary and Yugoslavia. The train soon slowed to a halt and the border guards got on. They asked us to show them our passports. Looking through it, he asked where we were headed for. I showed him our ticket to Istanbul. 'No, no,' he said, 'Get off the train.' We picked up our bags and got off.

WHAT A WAY TO TRAVEL

Standing on the platform, there was nobody else out there. Steve asked, 'Do you think we are being arrested?' I answered, 'I don't know, but something is seriously wrong. But they had better sort it out quickly otherwise the train is going to pull out without us onboard and God knows when the next one will be along.'

Suddenly at the opposite end of the train the man who had thrown us off was beckoning us to come to him. We picked up our bags and ran the whole length of the train. When we reached him he we were asked to follow him into the office. The man behind the counter had our passports, which he stamped with 'Expelled'. Giving our passports back to us he said, 'No Visas.' I told him we were not staying or stopping in Yugoslavia but we were in transit to Istanbul and would not be getting off of the train. 'Follow me,' he said, and off he went with us close at his heels and we entered another train. He showed us into a compartment and asked us to stay there. Steve and I looked at each other. We were both totally wiped out, our plans shattered. Just then the train we were on pulled out, heading for Istanbul. We just sat there, speechless. Then our train pulled out and we had no idea where we were headed for. Just then a ticket guard appeared at the compartment sliding door. He asked to see our tickets so I showed him my ticket to Istanbul. 'No, no,' he said, 'You need a ticket from here to Budapest.' Well, at least we now had been told where we were heading for. I went on to explain what had happened to us in Yugoslavia. He was totally disinterested. He used his calculator and came up with a cost in Hungarian money. I told him we had no Hungarian money so he calculated it in English pounds. Approximately £24.00. I told him, 'No way, I have just paid £120 for a ticket which is worthless.' He started to get quite verbal. I was so angry from all that had happened to us that I stood up and blasted him about everything that was on my mind. In the middle of the full-scale argument an angel appeared from the next carriage. She was stunningly beautiful and spoke perfect English. She asked what the problem was. I told her everything that had happened to us while in Yugoslavia and told her what the guard wanted from us. She had a go at him in Hungarian and he waddled off with this tail between his legs. We thanked her and she told us if we needed her again she was only next door and would be only too pleased to help if she could. That certainly warmed the cockles of our hearts. Perhaps today would not turn out to be too bad, after all.

Sitting there, I asked Steve what he had thought of Yugoslavia. 'Well,' he replied, 'At least I've been there, if only for five minutes.' At last we began to smile. Mind you, it was short-lived. The ticket guard reappeared. He said, 'You give me ten pound no ticket but I won't say anything and will let you stay on the train.' I looked at Steve and said, 'Let's just do it so we can get some peace around here.' We told him 'OK' and went to give him the £10.00. 'Not now,' he said, 'When we get nearer to Budapest.' It was pretty obvious that money was going to go straight into his back pocket. Well, he did come back later and collect his £10.00. Soon after, we arrived back in Budapest. Nothing ventured, nothing gained and that is exactly what we had got – nowhere – but we had overcome adversities before,

WHAT A WAY TO TRAVEL

so enter plan B. We changed £10.00 up and asked a cab driver how much it would cost to get us to the airport. We said about 1,200, and that is all we had. No more, 1,200 maximum, OK. He got out and put our bags and food into the boot. We all got in and zoomed off. He must have thought he was Nigel Mansell. He was a mental driver and he only had a Lada. But he took corners on two wheels. We were being thrown around all over the place. I turned to Steve and declared that at least we would not starve. Steve said, 'Hey?'. I replied, 'Well at least we've got food in the Lada,' being as the food was in the boot. We were rolling with laughter until we went over a bump and banged our heads on the roof of the car. This guy overtook anything that moved. We were just so glad to reach the airport. Unfortunately, the fare came to 1,400 but we only had the 1,200. He was none too happy as he threw our luggage out of the boot and on to the floor. Then he zoomed off.

We wondered why so many things were going wrong today. Surely our luck would change. We entered the airport and went to the information desk. The next flight to Istanbul was not until tomorrow afternoon. 25 hours away. We went back outside the airport and decided to sit down and look at our options. We could book the flight tomorrow, go back to the city, which would mean another £10.00 taxi drive, book a hotel for the night, plus we would need money for food and also a taxi back to the airport. Or we could book the flight and stay around the airport until the flight departed. It was the cheapest option and we had enough of keep going to Budapest. So, decision made, we went back inside to book the flight. The news we received was not what we wanted to hear. There was only one available seat on the flight. Steve and I retired back outside. We both agreed that perhaps we are not meant to get to Istanbul. This trip there just seems to be so many obstacles. Perhaps somebody is looking after us and it is not meant to be this time. We also agreed that we wanted to get out of here. Going back into the airport we noticed a flight to Copenhagen in Denmark which was due to leave in two hours' time. I said to Steve that we should check it out. They had seats available in business class so, although more costly, it would take us away from all of this. So we asked the check-in girl to book us in. We were given a complimentary drinks voucher and free drink on board the flight and as much as we wanted, and that is exactly what we did. We got hammered and put the whole experience our of our minds, and so were we! Steve had never been to Scandinavia before so this was a bonus for him and for me this was where all my travels started.

DENMARK - COPENHAGEN/ SWEDEN - MALMO

A shuttle bus service took us to the city centre from the airport. We asked a few passers-by about hotels and they directed us to the information bureau. Inside we discovered quite a unique system for getting tourists into hotels. All the hotels are listed, and then on a rotation system the bureau telephones the next hotel on the list if they have a vacancy for your particular requirements, then the booking is made, which saves you pedalling around the hotels. You pay the bureau a standard fee, the price of which is deducted from your hotel bill. This acts as their commission. It is that easy. Within minutes of arriving

WHAT A WAY TO TRAVEL

our hotel was all booked up, we were given a street map and directions and were soon settled into our room. It had been a long day, what with getting up at 4 o'clock, travelling through three countries, and all that free beer on the plane. Steve and I were happy to call it a day. So we got into bed and went out like a light. Waking up the following morning we felt brilliant. We were determined to enjoy ourselves and, after a good substantial breakfast, we set off for our city tour on foot. Our first stop was the famous Tivoli Gardens and, as luck would have it, this year was the 150th anniversary. It is a park full of amusements and rides, an open-air stage where stars perform, a cabaret theatre and a concert hall. There are over 28 restaurants to choose from which are beautifully situated at various points in the gardens. There is also a real frigate lying at anchor on the Tivoli lake. Leaving Tivoli we crossed the road through the main square over cobbled streets and right down the main shopping centre, viewing the articles for sale as we progressed. We soon reached the canal with its new and old sailing ships. Along both sides of the quaysides lie these incredible four-storey high houses with their quaint little windows all in a row and a multitude of colour for each separate house. It is very picturesque, with the long canal, still water and open canal sightseeing boats coming and going. We walked the entire length of the canal, enjoying the many vessels and people milling around. Right at the bottom of the canal on the left-hand side is the old Hans Christian Andersen museum which was unfortunately closed, but it is said that he lived around the area and wrote many stories from here. We carried on to the main sea inlet and watched many boats, ships and other vessels ferrying away on the waterway. Some huge ships were docked along the quayside for repairs, refurbishment or simply loading. One was the Vistaford, a ship I had sailed on around the Caribbean. We then walked through a park and found an amazing statue and water fountain. It was of a chariot pulled by four oxen with a lady driver who held a whip in her right hand pulled across her chest. But the water was sprayed across the wheels, giving the impression of motion through the water. We posed for our photographs alongside her but if you go to the bottom of the water fountain and look upwards, which is some 50 feet to the statue, there is a beautiful, layered waterfall with jets of water squirting over the surface. So we lay outstretched on the wall with the statue and fountain as a backdrop for another photograph. Leaving the park we went back to the sea inlet and followed the pathway. Not very far along there is the statue of the Little Mermaid sitting on the rocks just out in the water with rocks all around her. I love this statue as I think she is absolutely beautiful. To me she symbolises total purity, innocence. A mermaid from the sea with her human body and fish tail sitting on a rock, just warming herself from the sun's rays. Her head faces to the right and her legs are gently folded under her and, as we sat and looked at her with the water behind her and a clear blue sky, my mind went back to 30 years ago when I was a small ten-year-old boy and how excited I was at seeing the mermaid on the rock, and how determined I was at that age and height to touch her, and I did. Even though her foot, the lowest part of her, is some five feet off of the most jagged and slippery rocks and she sits about three feet high. We sat there for over an hour watching the coachloads of tourists arrive one after the other. Hordes of people arrived from all parts of the world, most snapping away with their cameras, group photographs, individual photographs, couples, families, young and old, some climbed on the rocks to be photographed next to her, some just to touch her, others falling in the water or slipping on the rocks. We also got involved, being asked to take many photographs of people. It was a great way of meeting and having conversations with all types of people from many different and varied backgrounds, plus boatloads of people viewing from the sea inlet on open boats. We waited for the right opportunity when hardly anybody was about when I moved in for my first photograph. I climbed on to the rocks and, touching her with my right hand, I said 'Hello' to her and asked her if she remembered me some 30 years ago. I like to think that she said 'Yes'. I also asked her if she would mind if I kissed her. I think she was flattered. I had observed her for over an hour, with hundreds of people coming and going, and although they photographed her and wanted to be photographed with her, nobody spoke to her or cuddled her or even kissed her and, believe me, she is real and she stands for all those that believe in the great ocean and seas that mermaids do exist. So I waded through the icy water, climbed the slippery rocks and hauled myself up on to the large rock that she sits on. Placing my left arm around her shoulder, I planted a loving kiss on her lips and told her I hope to see her again one day. As I started to climb down I suddenly realised those standing on the bank watching were clapping. I felt a bit silly, but proud. Steve, not to be outdone, also climbed up for a photograph and, believe me, the photograph turned out to be totally superb. Well, my last thought before leaving the Little Mermaid was that this was my start place for all of my journeys and I wondered that if by revisiting this area would this be the last of my travels? I would like to think that it is not but that particular moment is when I got my inspiration to write this book. I now had a start place and, coincidentally, the same place for the finish point, and within myself I felt great. We stood up, waved to her and walked away, looking back just once and we disappeared into the park.

Our next stop was an old war museum. It was brought to our attention by a home-made armoured car. The underground movement of local Danes made it. So we ventured inside to be met by an incredible collection of war memorabilia, guns, bullets, radios, clothing, maps and an amazing collection of photographs and newspaper reports. There was also a collection of torture tools. They looked ghastly, and to think that they were used on people is sickening. There was also a piece of human skin pickled in a jar with 'SS' tattooed on it, standing for the Nazi Secret Service. The one thing that really struck in my mind was an original Nazi flag with the swastika on, which had been half burnt. I wondered what sights and sounds it had experienced and how it ended up and how it has survived to this day, and maybe for many years to come.

Leaving the museum it made us realise the sacrifices some people made for others to live. Going through the exit we noticed a glass cabinet full of little brass mermaids sitting on rocks. I had to have one, and the Little Mermaid now sits with pride of place

WHAT A WAY TO TRAVEL

amongst my collection of ornaments. We walked back through the old Parliament Square and watched the uniformed guards parade with their rifles up and down. Well, it had already been a long day and we felt as though we had already packed a great deal of activities into the day and now it was time for something to eat, so we headed for the main shopping area. It is a very busy and active street. We were still there when darkness descended and the street takes on a new dimension. Street performers and entertainers filled the streets, men on one-wheeled bicycles doing juggling acts such as flame-lit torches, massed crowds gathered and the emphasis was on humour. There were singing acts, dancing, musical, puppet theatre, old and young doing their thing, but one act to me really stood out. It was a guy dressed as a clown but on stilts. He would wait around a corner and surprise unexpected passersby by bending down then standing up straight – with his height he would tower over them. He could spin around, dance and cock his leg backward over his head. The entertainment was fascinating and fun to watch. Our last visit of the day was to the red-light district. To say the least, it was mind-boggling and certainly an eye-opener. After all we had done today it was not 'hard' to sleep.

Well, another new day and another country to visit. We walked back down by the canal and caught a high-speed catamaran to Malmo in Sweden. It was only a 45-minute crossing and cost just £5.00 each for a return journey. The crossing was extremely smooth and the weather changed from a cloudy day in Denmark to a bright, sunny day in Sweden. As soon as we arrived we noticed a quieter and slower pace of life. A huge map of Malmo with the name made for a good photograph sitting under it. We crossed a bridge and noticed how clear the water was; so clear there was an abundance of jellyfish swimming in the water. A small local battery train ferried people around the shopping streets. We walked the whole length of the shopping avenue, there and back, enjoying going in the different shops to see what was on display. We took a picnic lunch in the main square under a huge statue of a horse's arse. Well, you have to admit it is a bit different.

We returned to Denmark, Copenhagen and spent our last night around the city centre. We had a superb send-off, being as Tivoli was celebrating its 150th year, a super fireworks display exploded over the gardens. It was a lovely ending to a super trip.

Next morning we caught a train right across Denmark to Esbjerg. On the journey the whole train was broken into sections and loaded on to a ferry. It seemed strange being on a train on a boat in the water. We eventually reached Esbjerg and, as luck would have it, a ship was sailing to Harwich in less than two hours. The journey would take twenty hours so it meant sleeping on board ship in one of the many mixed dormitories. Arriving in the UK, a train took us home. HOME, SWEET HOME. Some say it is nice to go away but it is better to come home. I agree, but I come home and make plans so I can go away then come back home again.

LIVING ABROAD

ITALY - PERUGIA/AMERICA - ORLANDO

Living abroad gives you a great opportunity to experience the way of life of the locals but at a leisurely pace of life. After meeting a Chinese lady in China called Ching Ching we corresponded for a couple of years and the occasional telephone call. The opportunity arose to go and stay with her in Perugia, Italy, where she was studying Italian at University. I took a flight to Rome, which proved the flashcubes in the Trivoli Fountain worked, promising one day I would return. The reunion at the airport was fantastic, kissing and cuddling. It was great to meet up with Ching Ching again. We stayed the first night in a hotel in Rome. When we last met she was struggling to speak English and now after only a couple of months she was speaking fluent Italian. The following day we took a train to the old historical town of Perugia. Being a university town the whole place was inundated with students and that is the type of life I lived for three months. Taking my meals at the university, joining the coffee sessions and lively debates with students from all over the world, meeting Ching Ching's fellow students for days our or family meals, going to bars or sharing a pizza in a restaurant. Ching Ching had booked me my own room and it was super inviting people around from very different backgrounds and enjoying a meal and drink and talking on all types of topics. It was so refreshing getting their views, ideas and opinions on world subjects. Ching Ching and I became very close, sharing everything including her Italian lessons. When I left Italy we planned on a trip of Ching Ching coming to England but, what with my commitments and hers, we have never quite been able to match up times, but I do live in hope. In the year 2000, she did come to England.

Another lady friend was Dianna from America. She lived in the Orlando area of Florida. I remember organising my bills at home and set off for the USA for a six month period. I was staying in Dianna's apartment with her and her eight-year-old daughter, Tyler. It was fun in the sun; the apartment was within a complex which had its own outdoor swimming pool and sunbathing beds. Many a day was spent lying on the beds in 90 degrees-plus and floating in the warm water of the pool, soaking up the rays and getting the best tan I have ever had. We spent our days shopping and visiting parks, going to the beach, visiting friends and families. We also went roller skating, to a circus and, through Tyler's friends and their parents, we went on many trips and functions and quite a few parties. A friend of mine joined me from England for a few days, which we spent in Epcot Centre and Wet 'n Wild.

The other side to living with friends in their country is you get the opportunity to invite them to come and stay with yourself and your own country. Dianna has stayed here already on a couple of occasions and plans to return soon, and this time she hopes to bring Tyler with her. On previous visits she wanted to see the Tower of London, Tower Bridge and St Paul's Cathedral but a must for her to photograph were a red bus and telephone box, a policeman, a black taxi cab and a good old red pillar box. Strange, but that is tourists for you!

I will leave you with a funny story. One day Dianna, my brothers and I were looking in a shop window, when a pigeon above pooped on her coat shoulder. I told her that in our country it is said to be lucky. She asked why was that so. So I told her it was lucky for us because it had hit her and not us! But most of all she enjoyed my friends' company and hospitality.

THE OLD ANCIENT WONDERS OF THE WORLD

MY PERSONAL CHOICE OF THE NEW WONDERS OF THE WORLD

These were the seven ancient wonders listed by Philon: -

- the Pyramids of Egypt
- the Hanging Gardens of Babylon
- the Statue of Zeus in Olympia
- the Temple of Artemis at Ephesus
- the Mausoleum at Halicarnassus
- the Colossus of Rhodes
- the Lighthouse at Alexandria

The only country area that I have not been to from the above are the Hanging Gardens, so that would go on my list of places still to visit.

MY SELECTION
- the Taj Mahal, Agra, India
- Acropolis, Athens, Greece
- the Palace, the Golden Buddha Complex in Bangkok, Thailand

WHAT A WAY TO TRAVEL

- Tutankhamun's Museum, Cairo, Egypt
- the Pyramids and Sphinx, Giza, Egypt
- the Great Wall of China, Forbidden City, Beijing, China
- the Terracotta Warriors, Xian, China
- the Little Mermaid, Copenhagen, Denmark
- the Eiffel Tower, Arc de Triomphe, Paris, France
- the Water Fountains of Barcelona, Spain
- the Golden Roof, Innsbruck, Austria
- Vienna, Austria
- the Colosseum, Forum, St Mark's Square, Italy
- the Spanish Steps, Trivoli Fountain, the Vatican, the Sistine Chapel, Rome, Italy
- Florence, Venice, Italy
- Dubrovnik, Yugoslavia
- Ephesus, Turkey
- Jerusalem, the Church, Wailing Wall, Dome of the Rock, Bethlehem, Church of Nativity, Israel
- Tulip Bulb Fields and Windmills of Amsterdam, Holland
- the Casino and Palace of Monte Carlo and Monaco, France
- the Statue of Liberty, World Trade Centre, New York, USA
- Disneyland, California, Disneyworld, Florida, USA
- most bridges in the world especially Golden Gate Bridge, Alcatraz, Las Vegas, Hoover Dam, USA
- the Statue of Christ the Redeemer, Rio, Brazil
- the Berlin Wall, Brandenburgh Gate, Germany

WHAT A WAY TO TRAVEL

- Red Square, The Kremlin, St. Basil's Cathedral, Moscow, Russia
- Sydney Opera House and harbour, Australia
- Hong Kong harbour
- the Temples of Kyoto, Japan
- Stonehenge, Dorset, England

MOTHER NATURE'S NATURAL WONDERS

Containing most of the mountain ranges of the world, snow, ice, seas, oceans, lakes, valleys, peaks, caves, plants, forests, trees, flowers, animals, birds, fish, insects, deserts, beaches, waterfalls, but a special mention must go to:-
- the Grand Canyon
- Niagara Falls
- Everest
- Mount Fuji
- the Alps
- the Algarve
- Rock of Gibraltar
- the Norwegian Fjords
- the Underwater World of the Great Barrier Reef
- the Dead Sea
- icebergs, volcanoes, geysers, thunder and lighting, other plants and the sun

WHAT A WAY TO TRAVEL

FAMOUS RIVERS
- the Nile
- the Danube
- the Seine
- the Rhine
- the Amazon
- the Yangse
- the Colorado
- the Mississippi
- St. Lawrence
- the Ganges

FAMOUS BEACHES
- St Tropez
- Miami Beach
- Palm Beach
- Wakiki Beach
- the beaches of Honolulu
- Paradise, Bali
- the Caribbean
- Bondi Beach
- Gulf of Siam
- and the many beaches of Europe and Asia

WHAT A WAY TO TRAVEL

MAN-MADE TECHNICAL WONDERS
- Aeroplanes like jets, jumbos, helicopters, Concord, space shuttles, rockets
- the bullet train
- Hydrofoils, ships, cruise liners, especially the QE2

SOME MODES OF TRANSPORT I HAVE BEEN ON
- tandem bicycle
- three-wheeled bicycle combination
- tuc tuc
- three-wheeled motorcycle
- coach
- bus
- mini bus
- car
- mobile home
- steam train
- electric train
- Metro
- tube
- ships
- cruise liners
- ferry boats
- high-speed catamaran
- cable cars
- ski lifts
- skis
- horse-drawn carriage

- and, of course, the camel
- and elephant

If you were to ask me my favourite place, memory, monument or landmark it would be extremely difficult to answer. Each one had its own special and unique individual charm and charisma. But if I was pushed and had to choose one I would have to pick the Church of Nativity, Bethlehem, Israel and the Star of David, said to be the manger in the stable where Christ the Lord was said to be born. Just for the impact it had on me at the time and how humble and privileged I felt afterwards, but I have many favourite and brilliant memories that will last my entire lifetime.

FUTURE TRIPS TO PLAN

1. Finland/Helsinki down through Romania, Bulgaria into Turkey/Istanbul/Gallipoli/Troy across to Crete and on to Malta.
2. Fly to Miami, cruise the Caribbean stopping at the Bahamas, St Kitts and Nevis, Antigua and Barbuda, Dominica, Martinique, St Lucia, St Vincent, Barbados, Grenada, Trinidad and Tobago and Venezuela/Caracas. Fly back to New Orleans, up to Memphis and Nashville, down to Dallas and the Alomo through Mexico to Mexico City and finally on to Acapulco.
3. See more of Africa. Perhaps a safari in Kenya or a trip down to South Africa /Johannesburg/ Cape Town then across to Madagascar, Mauritius, Seychelles and finally to the Maldives.
4. Flight into Burma, across to Vietnam across to the Philippines down to Papua New Guinea then on to the Great Barrier Reef in Australia and out through islands such as Fiji, Tonga, Western Samoa.
5. I would like to visit the area of the Hanging Gardens of Babylon and a trip to North and South Korea and, of course, if possible the North and South Poles and a trip right through South America.

WHAT A WAY TO TRAVEL

HOLIDAY TIPS AND PREPARATION BEFORE THE OFF

1. Tip number one, always travel light. Do not pack coats and heavy jumpers or cardigans. You can always put on extra T-shirts and remember – the weather abroad is not like our own. Take a light rain mac. But remember you can always buy little extra bits of clothing while abroad.
2. The only other items you will need are your passports, tickets, money, sometimes local money, a credit card and/ or travellers cheques, a camera and film. Always take a note pad and pen, sunglasses, sun cream and half a roll of toilet paper and, finally, do not forget to pack your swimming costume and towel.

OUR HOLIDAY SONGS

A) We're all going on a summer holiday
B) Always look on the bright side of life
C) Wherever I lay my hat that's my home
D) We are sailing
E) Don't worry about a thing because every little thing is going to be all right
F) Planes and boats and trains
G) Here we go again that feeling
H) Don't worry, be happy
I) The sun has got his hat on, hip hip hip hooray
J) and my favourite - Pick yourself up, dust yourself down and start all over again

GUARDIAN ANGEL MY ST CHRISTOPHER
(PATRON SAINT OF TRAVEL)

When I was a child my imaginary friend was Peter. I saw him. Mum had to give him his own chair and she even had to feed him.

Was it him with me on my travels? Let us look at some of the instances as, while travelling, to me they are like mini miracles.

- My safety as a child traveller, always finding accommodation at the right time and places.
- The mysterious guide appearing at Cairo airport and even just getting to Cairo.
- The ski instructor who just appeared and saved us from injury.
- The glass smashing on my girlfriend's head in Spain.
- The honeymoon and the sea incident.
- Meeting the American philosopher on Greek Gods
- The brothers in Delhi, India
- The ginger-haired man
- The guy in Paris with the tickets
- The man in Portugal with the villa
- Jim in Gibraltar

WHAT A WAY TO TRAVEL

- Chicago Joe in Morocco
- The porter on the train
- Angel on train in Budapest

And especially the Americans: JIM, DIANNA, TYLER, KELLY, TRACY AND BILL

THANKS FOR THE MEMORIES